<u>Time</u>
Management

BEST PRACTICES:
Time
Management

SET PRIORITIES TO GET
THE RIGHT THINGS DONE

JOHN HOOVER

8/07

Collins

An Imprint of HarperCollins*Publishers*

Produced for HarperCollins by:

HYLAS PUBLISHING
129 MAIN STREET
IRVINGTON, NY 10533
WWW.HYLASPUBLISHING.COM

FIRST EDITION
Library of Congress Cataloguing-in-Publication Data has been applied for.

ISBN: 978-0-06-114563-6
ISBN-10: 0-06-114563-7

07 08 09 10 11   RRD   10 9 8 7 6 5 4 3 2 1

John Hoover is a former executive with Walt Disney Productions and McGraw-Hill and holds master's degrees in marriage and family therapy and in human and organizational development, as well as a Ph.D. in human and organizational systems. Dr. Hoover is a leadership coach, organizational communications specialist, organizational behavior consultant, workshop leader, and keynote speaker for organizations, including the American Society of Training and Development, the Boeing Leadership Center, Delta Air Lines, IBM, Motorola, the New York State Training Council, the Society for Human Resource Management, Xerox, and many others.

He is also the author and coauthor of 12 management and motivation books, including *Bullwinkle on Business: Motivational Secrets of a Chief Executive Moose, How to Work for an Idiot, How to Live with an Idiot, How to Sell to an Idiot, The Art of Constructive Confrontation, Unleashing Leadership, Leadership When the Heat's On* with Danny Cox, and *Time Management* in the Collins Best Practices series.

Contents

Preface

Why do some people manage their time so effortlessly, while others are always behind? How can you stay on top of deadlines when obstacles crop up right and left? Is there a trick to moving ahead on long-term goals at the same time that you are dealing with your boss's last-minute requests?

In this book, we distill the wisdom of some of the best minds in the field of time management to help you make use of your time more effectively and achieve your long-term goals. The language is simple and the design colorful to make the information easy to grasp.

Quizzes help you assess your knowledge of time management. Case files show how people have addressed their own time-management problems. Sidebars give you a big-picture look at managing time effectively and highlight innovative, out-of-the-box solutions worth considering. Quotes from business leaders and expert time managers will motivate you as you try to make every minute of the day count. Finally, in case you want to dig deeper into time-management issues and other challenges of the workplace, we recommend some of the most important business books available. The authors of these books both influence and reflect today's thinking about managing time and related management issues. Understanding the ideas they cover will inspire you as a manager.

Even if you don't dip into these volumes, the knowledge you gain from studying the pages of this book will equip you to manage your time more effectively every day—to help you make a difference to your company and in the lives of the people who support you.

THE EDITORS

PRIORITIZE
YOUR TIME

"Time is the scarcest resource of the manager; if it is not managed, nothing else can be managed."

—Peter Drucker,
management guru and author
(1909–2005)

The 86,400 seconds in a day may sound like a lot, but they go fast. No matter how quickly time seems to fly by for you, even the most skilled time manager's hours, minutes, and seconds tick by at exactly the same rate.

Self-Assessment Quiz

HOW DO YOU PERCEIVE TIME?

Read each of the following statements and indicate whether you agree, somewhat agree, or disagree. Then check your score and study the analysis at the end.

1. Most of the things I do all day at work are mechanical and not personally gratifying.

   ○ Agree
   ○ Somewhat agree
   ○ Disagree

2. Most of the things I do all day are important to my employer but not to me.

   ○ Agree
   ○ Somewhat agree
   ○ Disagree

3. Most of the things I do all day are routine, and my employer doesn't really benefit from them either.

   ○ Agree
   ○ Somewhat agree
   ○ Disagree

4. At home, most of the things I do are routine and don't really benefit me or anybody else.

   ○ Agree
   ○ Somewhat agree
   ○ Disagree

5. At home, most of the things I do are important to other people but not to me.

   ○ Agree
   ○ Somewhat agree
   ○ Disagree

6. At home, most of the things I do are mechanical and not personally gratifying.

   ○ Agree
   ○ Somewhat agree
   ○ Disagree

7. My priorities are set by others at work.

   ○ Agree
   ○ Somewhat agree
   ○ Disagree

Self-Assessment Quiz

8. My priorities are set by others at home.

   ○ Agree
   ○ Somewhat agree
   ○ Disagree

9. If I had the choice, I would use my professional time much differently.

   ○ Agree
   ○ Somewhat agree
   ○ Disagree

10. If I had the choice, I would use my personal time much differently.

    ○ Agree
    ○ Somewhat agree
    ○ Disagree

SCORING

Give yourself 3 points for every question you answered "Agree," 2 points for every question you answered "Somewhat agree," and 1 point for every question you answered "Disagree."

ANALYSIS

23–30 You see yourself as a victim who has been robbed of control over your time. You don't feel empowered to set your own priorities or to determine how your time is used. As a result, much, if not most, of your time feels wasted.

17–22 You might be ambivalent about the demands on your time. You accept the fact that life is about compromise and have compromised yours out of necessity and apathy.

10–16 You have a healthy outlook on how to use time and keep your priorities straight. In your life, you maintain a healthy balance between work and play.

Some people seem to get so much more done. It's not because they have more time, however, it's because of their skill at time management. Managing your time will positively affect your daily output, your career and financial goals, and, ultimately, your success.

Behind the Numbers

THE WASTED HOUR

A manager earning $75,000 per year who squanders just one hour a day due to lack of organization costs an employer some $9,000 per year. Using the same formula, here's what other comparable time-wasters cost their companies:

Salary	Lost annual profit
$45,000	$5,625
$55,000	$6,874
$65,000	$8,125
$85,000	$10,625
$95,000	$11,875
$105,000	$13,125
$200,000	$25,000

If all of these managers worked for the same firm, they would drain $81,294 from the company's bottom line each year.

SOURCE: *The Organized Executive* by Stephanie Winston (Warner Books, 2001).

"Time is the substance of our lives," writes Alexandra Stoddard in her book, *Time Alive*. She explains that we don't create time in our lives but instead "create our lives in time." But people too often feel that, in their personal and professional lives, time is running them. They feel they only have time for one life—personal or professional—but not both. The difference in giving your time more meaning or making it more productive is not found in trying to speed up or

> "One cannot even think of managing one's time unless one first knows where it goes."
>
> —Peter Drucker

slow down your days. It is what you choose to do within the time frames that constrain us all that makes the difference. Are you taking advantage of the time that's available to you?

Some people seem to have been born with a natural understanding of time management. Fortunately for the rest of us, it's a skill that can be learned and developed. Leading organization expert and best-selling author Stephanie

The **BIG** Picture

PRIORITIES IN GOAL SETTING

Michael Gerber, the best-selling business author, explains that professional priorities are an essential element of a successful business. He believes that managers should set appropriate goals and then specifically choose to spend time on productive tasks that will help achieve those goals.

His bottom line: Don't waste time on things that don't bring more life to your business.

SOURCE: *The E-Myth Revisited* by Michael E. Gerber (Collins, 2005).

Winston claims that senior executives and CEOs seem to possess unique time management and organization skills that enable them to dramatically increase their productivity. Indeed, people who are good at managing their time have strong skills in several key areas. They have a clear vision of their big-picture goals at work and in life—long-term, yearly, monthly, weekly, and daily goals. They are skillful at breaking these goals down into smaller units, and they know how to translate these small units into action-oriented to-do lists filled with tasks. Finally, they understand that achieving long- and medium-range goals means crossing off every task they can on their to-do list, every day.

Ultimately, how well you manage time boils down to your level of personal motivation. How willing are you to learn from the mistakes you've made about using time in the past? How willing are you to go after the things you know are important to do for the future? Most people know what needs to be done; they even know how to do it. They just don't have their priorities straight at the moment they make decisions about how to spend their time. Being more efficient in the present will help you achieve the

• POWER POINTS •

THE ELEMENTS OF GOAL MANAGEMENT

Managing your time is predicated on setting and accomplishing your goals. These are the three elements of goal management:

- **Long-term goals** – These are the purposes toward which you direct your efforts. Typically, long-term goals are completed in a year or more.

- **Objectives** – These are the steps needed to achieve a long-term goal. Objectives are typically completed in a month or more.

- **Tasks** – These are the series of daily and weekly actions required to meet your objectives.

future of your dreams. First, however, you need to motivate yourself to change some of your thinking and your habits.

MANAGING TIME AND GOALS

In one sense, time management is about managing your goals. If you know what you want to achieve in the future, you can figure out how to use your time in order to get there. To help you get the right things done—that is, get where you want to go at work and in life—it's important to line up your daily actions and your long-term goals. Thus, the first step is setting the right long-term goals and then making sure your objectives and daily actions support those goals.

Goals

A goal is a purpose toward which you direct your endeavors. For example, your goal could be to increase your company's sales revenue by 15 percent. A soccer team's goal might be to win the annual championship. Another goal might be to earn an MBA degree.

There's an art to setting goals. The most effective goals are specific and measurable and should be motivating. If a goal is too vague— for example, the resolution to make your firm the "best company in the world"—you will not be able to monitor your progress toward that goal, or even know whether or not you have achieved it. Does the "best company in the world" mean "greater sales than any other" or "a greater return on sales than any other company"? Does it mean that your employee retention rate is the highest of the firms in your field? If the goal you articulate can't be measured, take another stab at defining it.

An effective goal is also ambitious but not impossible to achieve. For instance, a goal

Dos & Don'ts ☑

KEEPING YOURSELF MOTIVATED

It's important to keep your energy and motivation high when you're trying to improve your time-management skills. To avoid losing momentum, consider the following:

☐ Do write down your goals and post them in a prominent spot where you'll see them regularly.

☐ Do remember what you ultimately hope to achieve. Keep your eye on the prize, so to speak.

☐ Don't forget why you're doing what you're doing.

☐ Do work with a teammate who will keep you honest about your progress—and compliment you on your efforts.

☐ Do celebrate and reward yourself when objectives are met and goals are accomplished.

of earning an MBA within 6 months is not realistic; getting the degree within 2 or 3 years is reasonable. Assigning a reasonable amount of time for the completion of your goals is essential. Only if you've established a clear and realistic deadline will you be able to determine how to best accomplish that goal. How you define a long-term goal is, to some degree, up to you: Is it a goal you want to achieve in 5 years, 1 year, 6 months, or 3 months?

Regardless of what that time frame is, strong time managers break down their long-term goals into objectives. If your long-term goal is to finish a particularly complex project

• POWER POINTS •

THE BASICS OF GOALS

A goal is a purpose toward which you direct your endeavors.

- Goals should be specific and measurable.

- Effective goals are ambitious but not impossible to achieve.

- Assigning a reasonable amount of time to complete your goal is essential.

- To successfully achieve your goals, break them down into objectives and tasks.

within a year, for example, your objectives will state what you need to do in the next month, 3 months, 6 months, and so on to meet your long-term goal.

To move toward achieving these objectives, effective time managers break these objectives down further into tasks—things that you need

Outside the Box

THE BEST TIME

Some times are better than others for certain tasks. When the sun comes up, so does your blood pressure. With higher blood pressure, you're good to rise and shine. Your temperature goes up as well, and your metabolism gets ready for work as you do. At midday, your liver enzymes spring to action, ready to deal with your lunch. After dinner, your pineal gland cranks out melatonin, the hormone that makes you drowsy. You need to pay attention to your own body clock to determine which part of the day is best for you to make decisions, avoid making decisions, engage in physical activity, do your most creative thinking, and mentally process new information.

SOURCE: "Unwinding the Body Clock" by Dana Bauer, *Research Penn State* (October 7, 2004).

to do in the short term—within the week, the day, or the hour. This process of dividing a long-term goal into smaller segments is also known as chunking. Look at a goal as you would a big bar of chocolate. It's just not possible to stuff the whole thing in your mouth at once, even if that's your first impulse. So you break it into pieces: First, you divide it in halves or quarters, and then you break apart the individual squares. Most people eat the chocolate bar a square at a time—and it doesn't take long for the whole bar to disappear.

The most important thing to remember is not to obsess about your long-term goal, though you are thinking about it, discussing it as appropriate, and perhaps jotting down notes to yourself about it on occasion. This will help you remember the direction you're headed, as you focus on the chunks that you have determined will take you there. Keeping your ultimate goal in the back of your mind 'flavors' the chunks you're doing at any moment and gives them more meaning than they might otherwise have.

Remain focused on implementation and action. Achieve your tasks and objectives, and you'll hit the big target right where and when you're supposed to. As long as your goal-setting achieves the proper traction, you'll reach your destination, no matter how far down the road it is. When working toward your goals, remember the Eastern proverb that wisely states "a journey of a thousand miles begins with a single step."

Objectives

Objectives are smaller goals that must be completed in order to achieve a long-term goal. For example, the soccer team that wants to qualify

> "Don't say you don't have enough time. You have exactly the same number of hours per day that were given to Helen Keller, Pasteur, Michelangelo, Mother Teresa, Leonardo da Vinci, Thomas Jefferson, and Albert Einstein."
>
> —H. Jackson Brown,
> author of *Life's Little Instruction Book*

for the annual championship play-offs (their goal) must win enough games during the season. Winning each game is their objective. If they win enough games—that is, meet their objectives

• POWER POINTS •

THE BASICS OF OBJECTIVES

Objectives are incremental steps on the way to achieving a long-term goal.

- Failing to reach objectives jeopardizes the long-term goal.

- Reaching objectives builds confidence.

- Completing objectives on time keeps goal achievement on schedule.

during the season—the soccer team will achieve their long-term goal of making the play-offs. Reaching objectives moves you closer to achieving your long-term goals.

If you're responsible for the performance of others in your department or work area, you need to be sure your employees understand the long-term goals everyone is working toward. Then explain how the objectives you've set for each employee help to achieve those long-term goals. Describing how these objectives fit in the larger picture will give meaning and purpose to each employee's work.

When monitoring the progress of your employees' objectives, don't be too rigid. When someone is meeting objectives like monthly sales or production goals with aplomb, don't tell him, "That was great. Now give me 12 more weeks just like that one." The pressure might be too much and the bar set too high, leading the person to bail out emotionally. It's better to encourage the employee incrementally. Say, "Let's try for those numbers again next month."

Tasks

Reaching your objectives requires a series of actions or tasks. Tasks are the most specific steps needed to achieve an objective, and, in turn, a long-term goal. The amount of time required to complete a task can vary from a couple of hours to a couple of weeks.

In order for a soccer team to win games (objectives) and reach the play-offs (the goal), team members must practice before each game,

The BIG Picture

IT'S UP TO YOU

The only one who can decide whether you are using your time productively is you. Ask yourself: Are you achieving what you want for yourself and your family through your use of time? If the answer is yes, then you're managing your time well. But if you're constantly swinging into periods of frantic activity, you need to rethink your use of time and learn how to manage it more efficiently.

• POWER POINTS •

THE BASICS OF TASKS

Although tasks are the smallest increment in time management, they lead directly to the successful attainment of larger goals.

- Tasks are critical to achieving long-term goals.

- Tasks can be accomplished in a few minutes, hours, or days.

- Tasks must be taken as seriously as your larger objectives and goals.

- Tasks that seem intimidating should be broken down into smaller action items.

review the roster of players, and strategize accordingly. Winning a spot in the play-offs ultimately comes down to how well the team members accomplish these tasks. Tasks are actions that you can accomplish and check off. They give "traction" to objectives and, ultimately, to goals. Without tasks, you're spinning your wheels. Tasks help you catch hold of the pavement and move forward.

When goals seem overwhelming or intimidating, you break them into objectives. When objectives seem daunting, you break them into tasks. If a task seems too time-consuming or complex to tackle all at once, give some thought to how you can break it down into "action items"—items that can usually be completed within hours or a day.

Don't ignore or minimize the importance of tasks just because they're small. If you make a point of accomplishing each day's tasks, the big picture will take care of itself. If you tell yourself that you'll get a task or a certain number of tasks done by 10:00 a.m. and then succeed, the feeling of accomplishment is gratifying. You feel that much closer to achieving your objectives and reaching your ultimate goal, which is an encouraging feeling on its own.

PRIORITIZING

In our complex business world, you can't wait until you have reached one long-term goal before neatly moving on to the next. On any given day, you will be working on short-term tasks associated with multiple long-term goals and objectives. So how do you decide which to do first? You prioritize them.

But how do you decide which tasks take priority over others? Which tasks should be completed first, second, third, and so forth? The first step is to have a clear understanding of what's involved in each task by asking the following questions—who, what, when, where, why, and how.

Who? Who needs this to be done—your boss, a customer, a coworker, or a subordinate? Who will be performing the task? Who will benefit from this? Does the person asking you to do this task understand the demands it will make on your time and energy?

What? Exactly what are you required to do? Is it valuable in the big picture? Does the benefit of doing the job justify the investment of your time, energy, and resources?

When? By what date do you need to complete your task? Do you have the time to accommodate this request? Former president Dwight D. Eisenhower explained that truly important things are rarely urgent and urgent things are

BEING EFFICIENT VS. BEING EFFECTIVE

It's possible to be efficient without being effective. In other words, you can be busy without moving toward your goals. In order to determine whether you are using your time wisely, answer the following questions, "Am I efficient only at doing unimportant work? Am I busy just doing things, or am I getting things done?" To ensure that you are being both efficient and effective, it's critical that you match your priorities with the right tasks, and focus most of your attention on those things that will help you reach goals. That's time well spent.

THE BOTTOM LINE

Dos & Don'ts ☑

PRIORITIZING TIPS

If you are having trouble dealing with
your workload in a reasonable amount
of time, it might be time to consider
these tips. Followed routinely, they will
make a seemingly endless list of tasks
more doable.

- ☐ Do ask yourself the basics:
  Who, What, When, Where, Why
  and How.

- ☐ Do make lists and stick to them.
  According to experts, lists are
  one of the most effective time
  management tools.

- ☐ Do allow yourself more time than
  you think you need to perform
  necessary tasks.

- ☐ Don't let distraction sabotage your
  list of tasks.

- ☐ Don't forget to factor in time
  sinks like e-mail and returning
  phone calls.

- ☐ Don't fall into time traps like
  private net surfing or excessive
  chatting with coworkers.

rarely important. Unimportant things usually become urgent because of poor planning. Keep your priorities in mind as you take on new work.

Where? Are there any geographic differences that will have an impact on the timelines of the task you've been assigned? Are there time-zone differences, for example, that will need to be taken in consideration? If you are working with someone in a different office, state, or country, do you need to consider the time it will take to traffic communications or documents back and forth between those two locations?

Why? Why have you been asked to complete this task? Why is it necessary in the context of long-term goals? Understanding the big picture will help you stay focused and prioritize better.

Red Flags ✖◆

SIGNS OF POOR TIME MANAGEMENT

When a workplace is in a constant state of emergency, it's usually a result of poor time management. In managing your own time, be sure to anticipate the possibility that others may be operating in a state of chaos. Watch out for:

- Constant last-minute pleas to begin or finish projects

- Exhausted staff members

- Harried and harassed bosses

WORK **FLOW** TOOLS

MANAGING TIME BETTER

DEVELOP LONG-TERM GOALS

SET OBJECTIVES

CREATE A TO-DO LIST OF TASKS

TAKE ACTION

REPEAT DAILY

How? How should you complete the task? How will your completed task be measured or evaluated? "How" something needs to be done has a huge effect on time management decisions and on the quality and cost of the task.

> "We are far more productive than perhaps any other generation in history. We now have the tools—technological, strategic, and personal—that can help us in our efforts to manage our time, enhance our efficiency, and better manage our lives."
>
> —Marc Mancini,
> author of *Time Management*

MAKING LISTS

You've heard the advice a thousand times: "Write things down." Yet you still try to carry things around in your head. Busy, stressed-out managers are in a class by themselves when it comes to the number of important details or action items they need to be on top of. It goes with the territory.

Writing things down has a surprising benefit beyond merely helping you remember important information. After writing down your list of

Outside the Box

THE COMPUTER TO THE RESCUE

Computers and the digital age have given us the ability to do more—and keep track of more—than ever before. These are some of the benefits of using technology to manage your lists:

- Updating a list on a computer is faster than rewriting a list on paper.

- Knowing where your list is saves you the time of searching for it.

- Storing old lists digitally allows you to refer back to them if needed.

- Setting up e-mailer reminders—a feature of many programs—alerts you when something is due.

- Sharing lists with others is easy to do when lists are created and stored digitally.

what has to get done, you're more likely to experience a sudden "aha" moment about the best way to accomplish it and the order in which to get specific things done. That will help you do more in less time.

According to many time-management experts, writing down lists of tasks is the key to effective time management. Lists help you organize

Dos & Don'ts ☑

THE ART OF THE LIST

If you have more on your plate than you think you can deal with, making a list is the single most important step you can take in the planning process. A written record allows you to see it all in front of you.

☐ Do write things down.

☐ Don't try to rely on memory alone to remember important notes. Write them down on a piece of paper, which can always be referred to down the line.

☐ Do list your tasks in order of priority. Complete the most urgent tasks first and then get to other pertinent but less important tasks.

your goals, objectives, and tasks. Effective time management is less about saving time at any cost than about using the time you have efficiently.

Lists work on many levels. First, they are great motivators. Time-management experts know that almost nothing motivates most people more than crossing things off a to-do list. Second, lists improve your results. Without a list, it's easy to

- [ ] Do use your list as a reference when confronted with new tasks. You will have a good idea of exactly how much time you can dedicate to these assignments.

- [ ] Don't get bogged down by a seemingly endless list.

- [ ] Do make schedules using software programs such as Microsoft Office, which will send you an e-mail to gently remind you of an impending deadline.

- [ ] Do have a particular place where you keep your list so that it is easy for you and others to refer to it.

- [ ] Don't forget to remove tasks that have been completed from your list so they do not clutter the list of what still needs to be done.

forget all the small tasks that need to be accomplished toward reaching an objective.

Finally, lists make you feel in control. When there is a carefully planned strategic agenda, people have a road map for their time. Even more important, creating lists forces you to make decisions about how to use your time. The best lists are based on the priorities or relative importance and urgency of the things you need to accomplish. If you find yourself wondering how best to use your "now," check the list. If it's a sound and comprehensive list, the answer will be right in front of you.

With a good list, you won't ever have to rearrange your priorities on the fly. You won't have

• POWER POINTS •

THE BENEFITS OF LISTS

Writing down the things you need to accomplish as a to-do list offers many time-saving benefits, including:

- Prioritizing what is most urgent, second most urgent, and so on

- Showing other people what you're doing and how your time is spent

- Keeping you focused on the important tasks

- Providing a visual reminder of your long-term goals

to formulate plans during a crisis. Making lists also organizes your thinking, which is extremely important to effective time management. Scattered thinking wastes time.

Organized thinking, according to experts, is also the most creative and innovative thinking. Diane Deacon, president of the Creative Thinking Association of America, and Mike Vance, cofounder of that organization and the first dean of Disney University, the legendary training organization inside the Walt Disney Company, explode the myth that creativity comes out of chaos and disorder. On the contrary, they argue,

Plan B

KEEP YOUR FOCUS

Caving in to others' demands on your time can cause you to lose sight of your goals and derail them entirely. Do not become distracted by attending to everything and everyone around you. Remember what's important to you and what work means on your terms. Your time belongs to you first and foremost. If you're not careful, you can wind up so consumed by other people's business that you have no time left to accomplish your own goals.

SOURCE: *Time for Me* by Helene Lerner (Sourcebooks, 2005).

organization and well-ordered time management open up space and time for creativity.

Not only do lists help you get organized, they are a constant reminder of what you're working on and can improve how you communicate your efforts to others on the job. This is not to suggest that you should post all of your lists for the office—although shared electronic calendars on

• POWER POINTS •

MANAGE YOUR LISTS

It's one thing to create a to-do list of tasks, but quite another one to manage it effectively. To get the most out of your list, follow these suggestions:

- Arrange tasks in order of their importance and urgency.

- Rewrite your list as priorities change or fluctuate.

- Tackle your list by completing the first item on it, then moving on to the next one.

- Clean up and rewrite your to-do list every day before you leave the office.

- Take an upbeat attitude toward your tasks so that each one seems worthy of your time.

computers and lists for entire teams and departments are increasingly popular—but when a

Plan

ORGANIZATION AND CREATIVITY

Many people think that being organized and structured creates a rigid environment that stifles creativity and creative impulses.

Not so, according to authors Mike Vance and Diane Deacon. Creativity does not tend to flourish in a disorganized environment. This is where many team leaders and project teams go wrong. They approach a project in an unstructured manner in hopes that creativity and innovation will abound—only to be disappointed.

Creativity, innovation, and big results occur faster in an organized environment. For example, Disney Imagineers use "displayed thinking" or life-sized storyboards that cover entire walls to post ideas, draw correlations between them, and capture new ideas that spring from old ones. None of that would be possible without organizing the ideas first.

SOURCE: *Think Out of the Box* by Mike Vance and Diane Deacon (Career Press, 1995).

supervisor or coworker imposes a new demand on your time, consulting your to-do list will help you give a reasonable and realistic date and time for finishing the task. You won't need to guess. Although you can't tell your boss to adjust her priorities, you will have a ready answer when she asks if you're busy or if you can help: "Let's take a look at my to-do list and see what I can work out." It also avoids one of the most frustrating situations in business, which is to be over-whelmed with work without anyone else being aware of it.

The BIG Picture

DON'T JUST SAVE TIME—MANAGE IT

There is nothing on your to-do list that can't be accomplished with pro-fessionalism. Your motto should be: "Excellence everywhere and in all things." Put another way, if anything on your to-do list isn't worth doing with enthusiasm, why are you doing it at all? A positive attitude will make time seem to pass more quickly. So why not make the time-management deci-sion to make all your time, even time spent doing mundane tasks, quality time—that is, time doing a good job and doing it with a positive attitude?

How to Make a List

Making a list can be as simple as writing things down on a piece of paper and numbering them sequentially or as sophisticated as using a software program. Some software, such as

> "Highly productive people know exactly what they should be working on during their discretionary time. They break projects down into manageable pieces, so their short-term actions translate into long-term success."
>
> —Laura Stack,
> author of *Leave the Office Earlier*

Microsoft Office Suite Outlook, allows you to enter and schedule action items and set e-mail reminders of upcoming tasks. There are dozens of calendar, time-management, project-management, personal information management, and customer relations software programs that help you create and manage lists, designate priorities, and set up multiple reminders and alerts. People in your company's IT department can help you identify tools that would be particularly useful.

Some people prefer to jot their lists on yellow legal pads. Others print them out or program them into handheld devices. Most computerized or preprinted to-do list templates ask for the item or task to be done and when it's due. In other words, what's the time frame or deadline? There are also places for you to make special notations. If you're making your own to-do list, you can simply label the columns "Tasks," "When Due," and "Notes." That will cover just about everything you need to know.

Managers who are visually oriented sometimes use a dry-erase marker board and hang their list in clear view. You can easily update it, you can mark the priority items in red, you can refer to it easily if someone calls with a scheduling question, and, best of all, as you accomplish your tasks you can draw a line through them—a visible reminder that you are getting things done and moving forward.

The most important thing is to have a particular place where you keep your list, whether paper or electronic. You don't want to waste time hunting for your time-management list! Jotting notes on the backs of envelopes that get stuck in your pocket is not a good system. Neither is writing lists on loose sheets of papers that too easily disappear on your desk and can even be thrown away by mistake.

Day planners from Franklin Covey and other time-management presses, such as Day-Timer, are great organization tools, as are most pre-printed portable calendars. Keeping to-do lists on your personal digital assistant (PDA) or cell

UNFINISHED BUSINESS

Once you've decided to manage your time better, start by making a list of all your unfinished business. Write down every outstanding item—all that to-do stuff floating around in your brain—even if it's more than a hundred items: picking up your dry cleaning, purging old files, researching new ideas, and so forth.

Most people feel overwhelmed by the sheer number of items on that page—sometimes there are so many that you'd need to be superhuman to get it all done. The first step is to accept that some of the items won't ever get done without help. The second step is to prioritize the list and set a deadline for yourself. And finally . . . just do it.

SOURCE: *Get Organized* by Ron Fry (Thomson Delmar Learning, 2004).

THE BOTTOM LINE

phone allows you to access, organize, store, and work on your list on the run.

Wherever you keep your list and whatever form it takes, get into the habit of looking at it often. Review it first thing in the morning as well as every hour on the hour and—as almost all time-management courses strongly urge—before you go home at night, while your work is foremost in your mind.

Each time, update it and add to it, reprioritizing any tasks you haven't finished. At night, clean up your list by crossing off the tasks you've accomplished. Then rewrite the list with the tasks rearranged by priorities, especially if your priorities have changed. In the morning, you'll be prepared to dive right in.

MANAGING YOUR LIST AND PRIORITIES

Most time-management experts recommend ranking to-do items in terms of priorities. Once you've ranked the tasks on your lists, it's important that you start with the first item—the most important or urgent—on your list and only move to the next task when you've completed the previous one. If you usually take a list of tasks arranged in the correct order of priority, but then dive in at number five or six, you are not using your list effectively. Often people skip tasks high on their lists when they find them too intimidating. If that's the case, then these tasks haven't been sufficiently broken down into manageable bites; try breaking them into smaller chunks again. Also, remember that tasks high on your list are the most urgent. It might be wise to tackle them earlier in the day, when you have more energy and stamina.

"All work takes place in time and uses up time. Yet most people take for granted this unique, irreplaceable, and necessary resource. Nothing else, perhaps, distinguishes effective executives as much as their tender loving care of time."

—Peter Drucker

Managing the Variables on Your Lists

You are now primed to prioritize your tasks, put them on a to-do list and cross them off, and then go after what's next. But there is one more dimension to prioritizing your time: changing contexts. Things like financial imperatives, deadlines, other projects, and other commitments affect priorities. Anticipating rapid and unexpected changes can help you stay on top of things when your priorities shift.

Financial Priorities. Your financial priorities, which affect you and those who depend on you, both at home and in the workplace, are a major factor when you create a to-do list. If your company doesn't succeed financially, neither will you. Tasks on your to-do list must reflect the need to build financial stability for the enterprise. As conditions shift and economic threats appear, shift the emphasis of your tasks to help make the business more profitable.

• POWER POINTS •

ACCOUNTING FOR VARIABLES
All kinds of factors affect your ability to manage time effectively. You need to anticipate and be prepared for each of them:

- Financial concerns, both personal and professional

- Deadline priorities that change when you're not looking

- Issues with coworkers or subordinates at work

- Other projects that pop up

- Commitments inspired by obligation or a desire to avoid conflict

Deadline Priorities. Are the choices you're making about your time influenced by deadlines? Are these deadlines externally imposed,

> "There's nothing . . . NOTHING! . . . easier than writing a 50-item 'to-do' list. In which EACH ONE OF THE 50 ITEMS is truly of the Utmost Importance."
>
> —Tom Peters,
> management guru and
> founder of Tom Peters Company

self-imposed, or a combination of the two? Do the items on your list reflect someone else's agenda or your own? If deadlines change constantly as a result of someone else's poor planning or project volatility, renegotiate time frames so that nobody accuses you of constantly finishing late. In general, remember that whenever your job depends on contributions or direction from others, your timeliness is held hostage to their time-management habits as well.

Outside Influences. How do your coworkers, subordinates, and clients affect your to-do list? If the answer is, "More than I would like," consider

Dos & Don'ts ☑

GET IT DONE

After you've set goals and broken them into manageable objectives and doable tasks, all you need is a get-it-done attitude to move forward.

- ☐ Do tackle the hardest items in your to-do list first each day.

- ☐ Do multitask when necessary to stay current with your tasks.

- ☐ Do adjust priorities as necessary.

- ☐ Don't allow the tasks you don't complete to accumulate.

- ☐ Don't procrastinate; focus on how good it feels to accomplish tasks and dig in.

- ☐ Do invest energy and enthusiasm in your tasks when executing them.

- ☐ Do make a pact with yourself to follow through on your to-do list.

once again where you can best invest your time and energy to balance the interests of the company, customers, your career, and other people who matter to you.

> "If you wait until all the lights are 'green' before you leave home, you'll never get started on your trip to the top."
>
> —Zig Ziglar,
> motivational speaker

Other Project Priorities. When you take on a large project in addition to your job responsibilities, such as a philanthropic campaign, a cooperative effort with another company, or a project with a church, temple, or community organization, it's easy to be overwhelmed. Take a macro view, so that you clearly understand the bigger picture and portion out your time accordingly. No matter how big and overwhelming the project seems, it will become more manageable as soon as you break it down into chunks.

Conflicts and Commitments. How many of your priorities are based on commitments inspired by guilt, obligation, or a desire to avoid conflict? Completing these tasks may not be the best use of your time. To avoid conflict at the expense of time management is bad policy. Don't be afraid to say "No." Once you've set your priorities in the first place, stand your ground when others try to get you to change them against your better judgment.

GETTING IT DONE

When a project keeps expanding or contracting, it's helpful to keep priorities flexible. When you lay out goals and priorities, have a Plan B. For example, how often have you wasted time because you struggled unnecessarily with something that obviously needed to be delayed? If a thing near the top of your to-do list can't be done today, either break it into smaller chunks or reschedule it for another day, and move on. However, don't make postponing tasks a habit. Focus on how good it feels—rather than on how hard it is—to accomplish things, and dig in.

In *Leadership When the Heat's On,* Danny Cox advises that you make the first hour of your day your most productive by tackling the hardest things then. He also recommends looking at the items on your daily to-do list and prioritizing them according to the following criteria:

Do today no matter what: Items that absolutely must get done

Do today if possible: Items that ideally should be done

Do today if time remains: Items that can wait but should be done if time allows

Don't procrastinate. By making this pact with yourself to follow through on your to-do list, you will feel better and more efficient at the end of each day. You will avoid feeling guilty about putting difficult things off for another day. Consider, too, that hourly or daily tasks left uncompleted accumulate. Before you know it, unfinished daily tasks interfere with accomplishing weekly objectives. Unfinished weekly objectives muddy the waters for your goals to be reached. Executing the immediate tasks at hand sets the stage for executing your objectives and long-term goals.

The only way to achieve goals is one small step at a time. You must address these small steps in the moment. That makes the "now" priority number one. Use it or lose it.

ORGANIZE
YOUR TIME

"Anything becomes
urgent if you wait
long enough."

—Danny Cox,
author of *Leadership When the Heat Is On*

The efficient use of time can make all the difference between effectiveness and ineffectiveness. It is a natural outgrowth of organization, which makes the most of your time and energy.

Self-Assessment Quiz

YOUR ORGANIZATION I.Q.

Read each of the following statements and indicate whether you agree or disagree. Then check your score and study the analysis at the end.

1. I let mail accumulate.
   - ○ Agree
   - ○ Disagree

2. The horizontal spaces in my work area are so covered with stuff there's no space to work.
   - ○ Agree
   - ○ Disagree

3. People get annoyed because I never return calls or answer e-mails.
   - ○ Agree
   - ○ Disagree

4. I avoid socializing because I don't have the time or energy left to deal with people.
   - ○ Agree
   - ○ Disagree

5. I have piles or boxes full of things I will go through "when I get the time."

○ Agree
○ Disagree

6. I put off making decisions until the situations become emergencies.

   ○ Agree
   ○ Disagree

7. I have so many to-do lists that I don't know which one to do first.

   ○ Agree
   ○ Disagree

8. I feel uncomfortable hiring people to do things for me.

   ○ Agree
   ○ Disagree

9. I am so plagued by interruptions that I can't get anything done.

   ○ Agree
   ○ Disagree

10. The clutter in my life is so over-whelming I don't know where to begin sorting it out.

   ○ Agree
   ○ Disagree

Self-Assessment Quiz

SCORING

Give yourself 1 point for every question you answered "Agree" and 0 points for every question you answered "Disagree."

ANALYSIS

0–3   You are a relatively organized person. You deal with things promptly, know how to keep disruptions to a minimum, and have efficient routines.

4–7   There are some organization issues that you should face, but you're within striking distance of recovery.

While some people are highly organized, many people are drawn into chaos by the demands of work and of others.

In fact, they are so habitually disorganized and stressed that they feel they cannot invest the time necessary to bring order to their lives, no matter how much they need guidance.

But organizing yourself and your time is not as difficult as it seems and it will eliminate a great deal of stress. It involves creating systems—consistent ways of doing things. Systems transform your daily, weekly, monthly, and yearly goals, objectives, and tasks into a coordinated whole.

You probably go through cycles of disorganization, depending upon the amount of pressure you're under. You could benefit from some organization training.

8–10 You are so used to chaos that it seems normal. To prevent your life from running you instead of the other way around, start using the principles in this book.

SOURCE: *How to Get Organized* by Stephanie Culp (Writer's Digest Books, 1986).

They create consistency, and consistency saves time. If, for example, you know exactly how you're going to get ready for work in the morning or how you're going to process e-mails when you arrive at work, you'll do these tasks with less time and effort than if you reinvent the wheel every day. By developing systems—and then maintaining them—you will bring order to your day.

After you've identified what your priorities are, as discussed in Chapter One, you must have the discipline to do the things that represent the best use of your time and say no to the things that interfere. Structure in your daily affairs comes from thinking ahead and planning. It includes scheduling wisely, meeting deadlines consistently, and organizing yourself and those around you, including your team, boss, and clients.

SCHEDULING

For many working professionals, a day is an exercise in playing catch-up. You may be late for your

The BIG Picture

TIME TYPES

According to author Julie Morgenstern, there are many "types" of time. Which of these are most important to you?

- Work time is time allotted to earning money.

- Self time recharges your batteries and restores your physical, spiritual, and emotional well-being.

- Family time allows you to build and sustain relationships with the most important people in your life.

- Relationship time involves other people who matter to you—old and new friends, and collaborators on school, church, or civic projects.

- Financial time goes to financial planning, investing, budgeting, ten o'clock meeting because you had to respond to an urgent e-mail. The meeting itself runs too long. A crisis with a client interrupts lunch on the run. Before you know it, three o'clock rolls around and you are just barely getting started with the tasks that need to get done that day. The secret to avoiding chaotic days such as this one is effective scheduling.

dealing with bills and taxes, and so on.

- Community time is spent improving your community, in such ways as religious fellowship and serving the needs of the less advantaged.

- Education time is devoted to learning by taking classes, watching films, reading, or studying online.

You might have other types of time that are important to you: hobby time, exercise time, or travel time. Whatever they might be, understanding the different types of time will help you manage them and balance your life more effectively.

SOURCE: *Organizing from the Inside Out* by Julie Morgenstern (Owl Books, 2004).

Dos & Don'ts ☑

SOUND SCHEDULING

When you begin to make a detailed schedule, it is good to be aware of any pitfalls that may be lurking in the shadows. A good schedule is always prepared for and ready to accommodate surprises.

- ☐ Do be prepared for crisis and catastrophe. Schedule time for them.

- ☐ Don't forget to be flexible.

- ☐ Don't neglect to have a Plan B in case of unforeseen emergencies.

Scheduling is all about being prepared. Most problems or crises you face on a daily basis are rarely that much of a surprise. You probably have encountered them before: That weekly ten o'clock meeting always runs late and that particular client always threatens to go to your competitor after receiving the first cost estimate for a project. Proper scheduling takes into account all your on-the-job knowledge and experience to prevent expected—and even unexpected—problems from knocking you flat.

A good schedule is flexible enough to accommodate unforeseen developments and complications. Developments and complications

☐ Do assess your to-do list according to priority.

☐ Do become aware of how much time you need to complete certain tasks. This will help you better manage the time that you have.

☐ Don't try to get it all done in one day; instead, spread specific tasks over the course of a week.

☐ Do schedule time for thinking—a vital part of getting the work done.

that can be anticipated should never push the agenda off track. A good scheduler always has a Plan B. Creating a schedule that anticipates all possible snafus is critical.

Setting Up a Sound Schedule

The first step to creating a sound schedule is assessing your to-do list. If you've ranked the items on your to-do list according to their priority, then you'll have a clear idea of what tasks absolutely need to get done in any given week. At the beginning of the week, take a look at your to-do list and estimate how long it will take you to complete each task. If you aren't good at figuring

Outside the Box

SEIZE THE TIME

In 5 minutes, you can put a pot of coffee on to brew and, while you're waiting, check e-mail and voice mail, send a fax, and address an envelope and drop it by the mail room. The coffee won't brew any faster with you staring at it, so adopt a "Do it now!" attitude. Use the small spaces between the big things in your life to attack the little things that clutter your days. In this way, you'll consolidate chunks of time to tackle your really important goals.

SOURCE: *Time Alive* by Alexandra Stoddard (HarperCollins, 2005).

out how much time is needed to do various tasks, start keeping track of how long it takes you to complete each task, including any interruptions, and make a note to yourself for the future.

Once you've determined how long each task will take, plan when you will tackle them. Decide which day you will do item number one, number two, and so on, and plug the tasks into a daily planner or online calendar. Don't cram as many tasks as possible into the first day of the week. Instead, distribute the tasks evenly throughout the week, taking into consideration already scheduled meetings and deadlines for tasks.

Be sure to factor extra time in the day to complete daily activities, such as responding to e-mails and returning phone calls.

Always allow more time to complete each task than you've estimated. If you think a project will take an hour, give yourself an hour and 15 minutes or even an hour and a half. Remember that it doesn't take a crisis to gobble up time unexpectedly. Activities you forget to include in

DON'T WAIT FOR THE BIG IDEA

Author Jim Collins points out that great companies like Walt Disney and Hewlett Packard didn't start out with a single great idea. Their creators worked on one idea after another until several took hold. Then they poured out an endless stream of new ideas. If they had spent their time waiting for the one perfect idea instead of acting on their many reasonable ideas, these legendary companies would have never succeeded as they did.

Stop waiting for a big idea to launch you. Kick into action and trust that the organized time you're spending on routine ideas will set the stage for big ones.

SOURCE: *Built to Last* by Jim Collins and Jerry Porras (HarperBusiness, 2004).

THE BOTTOM LINE

your schedule will wipe out what you thought
was extra time in the margins of your day.

Troubleshooting Your Schedule

If, after scheduling daily and weekly tasks as sug-
gested above, you are still frustrated that you can't

• POWER POINTS •

CREATING A SOUND WEEKLY SCHEDULE

An effective schedule can restore
order to your day by building time to
complete expected and unexpected
tasks. Here are a few tips for creating
a sound weekly schedule:

- Assess your to-do list.

- Estimate realistically how long each
  task will take to complete.

- Build in extra time to allow for daily
  activities, such as responding to
  e-mails and phone messages, as
  well as unexpected interruptions.

- Factor in "thinking" time to strategize or work through an issue or
  problem.

- Distribute tasks throughout the
  week as evenly as possible, taking
  into consideration deadlines and
  other obligations.

Outside the Box

USE YOUR SUBCONSCIOUS TO SAVE TIME

Have you ever had "aha!" or "eureka!" solutions pop into your head days after you needed them? Begin to consciously delegate projects to your subconscious. When faced with a difficult decision or situation in which you are having trouble coming up with options, try to forget about it for the moment. When your mind is at rest, the answer will come. This is known among scholars as the incubator technique, or thought incubation. While the solution is incubating, use your time to continue work on another project.

SOURCE: *Taking Control of Your Thoughts* by Harrison Shorter (Harrison House, 2003).

blaze through your to-do list, you may not be accounting for distraction time. Almost any task is interrupted multiple times before it's completed. That's why conferences, special strategy sessions, and other activities that require intense focus are so often held away from the office. Theoretically, moving away from your base of operations reduces distractions. It also lends a certain air of enhanced significance to what you're working on.

Another reason you might not be able to complete your to-do list in a timely fashion is that you are not building in time to "think." Periods of concentration devoted exclusively to wrapping your mind around a major project or strategizing how best to respond to a problem are critical to executing tasks effectively.

Often, however, we postpone thinking about larger questions and issues until it's absolutely necessary. "I can't think about that right now. If I do I'll go crazy. I'll think about that tomorrow," sighs *Gone With the Wind* heroine Scarlett O'Hara. But if you bump your thinking from one day to the next, you might run out of time. Trying to produce a strong strategy or plan of execution without enough time to

THE TWO-LIST SYSTEM

Organizing expert and author Stephanie Winston suggests keeping two lists of tasks at all times: a master task list—a kind of a reservoir of "to dos"—and a daily to-do list. The key is to write any and every task that needs to get done on the master list, even if those tasks need to be done a month or two away. The daily to-do list details those tasks that must be done that day, organized according to their high, medium, or low priority. There's a good reason for prioritizing the tasks on your daily to-do list.

think it through might cause problems later down the line.

Whenever you schedule "thinking" time, be aware that you might require more flexibility in your schedule than is otherwise needed. When your brain says, "That's enough thinking for one day, let's switch to a less intense activity," do it. This may be the time to sort papers, do some filing, or clean out your e-mail.

Sometimes you may devote your thinking time to large questions and issues, but every day you should also set aside time to think about the next day's activities and demands on your time. This will ensure that you are better

A small task, such as filling the car with gas or picking up dry cleaning, may seem like a low priority in and of itself. But if you need to accomplish it before you can complete a high-priority task, such as going on a job interview, that may change the urgency regarding the first task. You can jot down your lists on a piece of paper or type them into an electronic document—but always keep the daily, scheduled to-do list handy.

SOURCE: *Getting Organized* by Stephanie Winston (Warner Books, 2006).

THE BOTTOM LINE

CASE *FILE*

TAKE-NO-PRISONERS TIME MANAGEMENT

The rebuilding of highways in Los Angeles after the Northridge earthquake in 1994 is a good example of take-no-prisoners time management. On January 17, the earthquake injured more than 9,000 people and damaged or destroyed 54,000 buildings, including the Santa Monica Freeway (I-10), one of the world's most heavily trafficked highways.

Rebuilding the freeway began less than 24 hours after the quake. When the contractor was told that it would take 3 weeks to ship steel beams to repair two fallen I-10 bridges, he

prepared to tackle the next day's tasks and allow you to reschedule any task that wasn't completed by the end of the day.

PROJECT SCHEDULES

A project is, in essence, a goal and should be handled accordingly: by breaking it into smaller objectives, creating and prioritizing a to-do list of tasks, and scheduling those tasks. When you schedule or draft a timeline for a project, you are creating a map that will tell you exactly how you will spend your time leading up to the project deadline.

chartered trains himself. He used quick-curing concrete, although it cost more, and rebuilt both bridges at once rather than in sequence, with laborers working 12 hours at a time and crews out 24 hours a day rain or shine. As a result, I-10 reopened in a lightning-fast 66 days. The contractors blew past all typical roadblocks—paperwork, supply issues, manpower—in a prime example of effective time management producing excellent results.

SOURCE: "Lessons for Post-Katrina Reconstruction" by Peter Phillips, Economic Policy Institute (October 6, 2005).

Completing your project on time is important, if only because inefficiency on your part can be contagious. Even the overachievers in your group might slack off when they realize you are not dealing successfully with your own deadlines. In addition, missing a deadline may mean that all the time, energy, and resources you spent on a project were wasted.

Setting Up a Project Schedule

The first thing you should do when scheduling a project is to assess how realistic its deadline is. As soon as you have been asked to complete a project within a given time, identify all the factors that could derail the project's timeline: Do you have the resources you need? Can vendors supply in time? How long will approvals take? Also consider: Who's done this before? Can it be done again faster? Who can teach me how to get this done on schedule? If, after considering these factors carefully, you feel the deadline is not reasonable, go back to your superior or whoever assigned the project to renegotiate the due date, if possible.

Once you've decided on a realistic deadline, it's time to create a timeline. The best way to schedule a project is by working backwards from

OUTSIDE HELP

At times even a well-organized, time-efficient department or project team comes up against a deadline that seems insurmountable. When this occurs, interns, temp workers, freelancers, or independent contractors are worth considering. Such outside help can take over busywork, leaving you and other project team members free for the most critical tasks. More experienced freelancers bring fresh ideas. They excel at breaking logjams, offering tested solutions and the project's due date to the present. Plot the sequence of tasks that need to be completed to get you to the finish line. These tasks may not always be evenly distributed throughout the course of the project, but rather grouped tightly together at certain intervals.

Take a cue from moviemakers, who rarely shoot scenes in the order the audience sees. Don't be afraid to complete tasks out of order. You may choose to finish the last piece of the project first and the third piece seventh if it will help you maximize resources and key players. Engage your team's help to determine what tasks can be done quickly and inexpensively and which

Plan

inspiring, as well as helping, you. Most critically, freelancers can help you accelerate your project schedule. Freelancers tend to be conscientious because their livelihood depends on referrals and repeat business. If you anticipate that you won't be able to meet your deadline with staff resources, don't wait until the eleventh hour. Ask your boss or the human-resources department for whatever outside resources you need and call in reinforcements.

Dos & Don'ts ☑

PROJECT SCHEDULING

Your upcoming project involves many steps, too many to remember on your own. After assessing your time and resources, make a step-by-step list that will take you seamlessly from start to finish.

☐ Do assess how realistic your deadline is.

☐ Do identify and anticipate possible roadblocks and setbacks.

☐ Do plot a project's sequence of events from start to finish.

☐ Don't be afraid to complete steps out of their chronological order.

☐ Do determine what tasks can be done quickly and inexpensively and which will take longer and cost more.

☐ Don't fritter away your downtime. Use it wisely.

☐ Do try and complete some tasks away from your regular workplace.

will take longer and cost more. Then, sketch out a reasonable sequence for things to happen. As you schedule the project, focus not only on the time it will take you to get these tasks done, but also on what you will do or what needs to happen during quiet periods—intervals in which no tasks need your attention.

If, after you've started your project and work is underway, you feel frustrated that you're not staying on schedule, you might not be accounting for these quiet periods, when little work gets done. If it feels as if your project is crawling at a snail's pace, it is important to review what can be done to minimize downtime and keep tasks moving.

Take the example of a project that involves creating new stationery for a corporate client. To speed up the project, you might limit your paper selection to stock that's available domestically. By eliminating paper that has to be specially ordered from Asia and takes a month to deliver, you're eliminating downtime during which nothing would be accomplished.

USING
YOUR TIME
EFFICIENTLY

"Saying 'No'
to someone else
is like saying 'Yes'
to yourself."

—Helene Lerner,
author of *Time for Me*

Everybody faces unexpected roadblocks that interfere with how they use their time. The difference between people who achieve their goals and those who fail is their skill at navigating around the roadblocks that threaten to stop them.

MANAGING DISTRACTIONS

Time traps such as too many e-mails, phone interruptions, poorly run meetings, and chatty coworkers can derail even the most sound schedule and wreck havoc with your to-do list. To deal effectively with these distractions, it's essential that you remain in control of your time and that you don't give in to people's attempts to impose themselves on your schedule.

This chapter will explore the many "time-traps" that you are likely to encounter throughout the workday and ways to avoid or counteract them.

Cope with E-Mail and Paper Overload

In today's wired workplace, hundreds of daily e-mails, instant messaging, and messages sent via

Dos & Don'ts ☑

AVOIDING E-MAIL DISTRACTIONS

E-mail has improved our work productivity by making communication faster and more efficient. But if not used effectively, e-mail can become one of the most dangerous time traps:

☐ Do delete junk e-mails right away as well as e-mails from lists you subscribe to but rarely read.

BlackBerries and other wireless devices compete for our attention. Technology has made communication easier and faster, but it has also buried us in information. In the past, handling correspondence was simply a matter of going through a stack of letters and memos. Now, it's not uncommon to receive over 50 e-mails a day that demand your immediate attention. Meanwhile, even as technology promised to bring about "the paperless office," we still receive plenty of hard copies of reports, memos, letters, and junk mail.

When you receive an e-mail or document, read it to evaluate whether it requires any action on your part. If you receive hundreds of e-mails a day, reading everything that shows up may be pointless. Master the "art of the glance" and determine what you can justifiably ignore. Learn to

- [ ] Don't read every e-mail right away. Scan over messages to determine which require immediate action.
- [ ] Do designate a specific time of the day to handle e-mails.
- [ ] Do respond to e-mails promptly.
- [ ] Don't let e-mails accumulate and clutter your inbox. Delete or file them after you've dealt with them.

• POWER POINTS •

AVOID MAIL CLUTTER

Your e-mail in-box chime goes off and there is something waiting for your attention. The postal carrier drops off a big stack of mail with a rubber band around it. It takes time to process that stuff. If your paper mail and e-mail are not managed well, they could swallow up all of your available time reacting to them. Stay in control of paper mail and e-mail clutter by:

- Not opening paper mail or e-mail the moment it arrives

- Making sure you do something with it within 24 hours

- Setting up a particular part of the day to toss, file, or respond to paper mail or e-mail

identify junk e-mails or messages from e-mail lists you subscribe to that can be immediately deleted.

Once you've determined whether an e-mail or document requires action on your part, take care of it. Respond to e-mails promptly. Be brief—by writing short, well-articulated e-mails, you will save time, and so will the e-mail's recipient.

The most important thing is to keep on top of your e-mail in-box; don't let e-mails that require immediate action accumulate. After you've responded to an e-mail, delete it or file it in an e-mail folder. Don't let the e-mails that you've already taken care of clutter your in-box and potentially hide other e-mails that still require your attention.

Similarly, once you've opened a piece of mail or received a document that you've

---

THE THREE "R"S

When e-mail and paper documents don't get handled efficiently, they pile up, disorganize your work area, and waste invaluable time. To keep e-mails from clogging your in-box and document stacks from growing, time-management author K. J. McCorry suggests adopting the three "R"s:

- Read it
- Respond to it
- Remove it

If you can't do one of these things with the e-mails and papers in your life, you don't have an organization problem, you have a decision-making problem.

SOURCE: *Organize Your Work Day in No Time* by K. J. McCorry (Que, 2005).

THE BOTTOM LINE

determined needs your attention, handle it as soon as possible. Don't toss it in a pile of "stuff" that needs to be reviewed and acted on. Not only will important papers get lost, but this pile can quickly grow to an unmanageable size and eventually take hours and hours to sift through. Once you are done with the document, toss it in the recycling bin or file it. Don't let it sit idly on your desk, taking up room and possibly distracting you from other important papers.

Some people find it useful to designate a particular chunk of their day to writing and responding to e-mails and paper mail. For example, you might decide to dedicate an hour

Dos & Don'ts ☑

TELEPHONE AND TIME

The phone is one of the most important communication tools, but it can also interrupt and distract you from more crucial things on your to-do list. Here are a few tips for using the phone efficiently:

☐ Do take important calls and schedule time for the rest.

☐ Don't go "off-line" or "silent" for such extended periods of time that people feel you are unresponsive. They'll just call more often.

or more every morning to writing and returning e-mails. That clears the rest of the day to work on tasks unrelated to e-mail. If you think this approach would work for you and for your particular job, try making it a routine. Knowing that you've dedicated a particular amount of time to dealing with your e-mail and papers will help you schedule your daily tasks and create a more realistic agenda for the day.

Manage the Telephone Trap

Although the telephone is a useful communication tool, it can become a problem when your phone habits fail to follow the principles of your time-management system. Incoming calls are

- [ ] Do use your cell phone and other wireless devices to turn dead time into productive time.

- [ ] Don't allow your cell phone or other wireless devices to interrupt a meeting. Set boundaries.

- [ ] Don't rely on Post-it notes to write down phone messages, which are likely to get lost or buried under other work. Keep a dedicated notebook for this purpose by the phone.

beyond your control; they can interrupt you in the middle of a task and derail your schedule. But whether you are receiving or making calls, adopt these tricks to save valuable time.

Avoiding the phone. One way to avoid phone interruptions is to not answer the phone when you are intensely focused on something important. Instead, schedule a time to check voice mail. That way, you're not ignoring people indefinitely, but you are protecting blocks of time from interruptions. When you go through

• POWER POINTS •

MANAGING TELEPHONE CALLS

Whenever your phone rings, someone is making demands on your time. If you're not careful, calls can waste enormous amounts of time. Here are some telephone management tips to remember:

- Plan your telephone strategy in advance.

- Don't answer the telephone until you're ready to.

- Return telephone calls at a pre-designated time of day.

- Tell callers right away how long you're willing to talk.

your voice mailbox, you will be able to screen unimportant calls faster and more easily than you could by picking up the telephone every time it rings.

Beware, though, of making a habit of always letting the phone ring without answering. If people, particularly clients or customers, realize that they can't routinely reach you by phone, they'll figure out another way to find you—probably by e-mail—and create another way to interrupt you.

Returning calls promptly. Of course, missing phone calls while you are at meetings, client calls, lunch appointments, and so on is unavoidable. Make sure your voice-mail greeting is friendly, but brief and concise. Specify what information

The BIG Picture

HIGH-TECH INTERRUPTIONS

Unfortunately, technology gives more people greater access to you and to your time. Keeping control of your time and your schedule means focusing on the priorities you've set. But it also means tuning out the things you don't need to be doing. Occasionally avoid e-mail, cell phone calls, the addictive handheld wireless device, and anything else that might take on a life of its own and detract from yours.

to leave. If you want the caller to reach you on your cell phone or at another number, say so. If there is a staff member who fields your phone calls, refer callers to that person. If you're not going to be returning calls until a certain time, state that clearly.

As with responding to e-mails, you might want to dedicate a particular time of your day to returning phone calls. Whenever possible, you want to return all calls by the end of the business day—phone messages that accumulate will

• POWER POINTS •

TELEPHONE EFFICIENCY

When you do dial the phone or accept a call, you still want to make efficient use of the time. It's tempting to relax and chat when there's a telephone receiver in your hand. To stay in control of telephone time, remember to:

- Avoid giving callers a chance to chat endlessly.

- Ask callers politely to get to the point.

- Give verbal cues when it's time to move on or end the call.

- Write out your talking points before you call.

The BIG Picture

CONFUSING SUCCESS AND SPEED

A common misconception is that time management is about fast, faster, fastest. Do you confuse success with speed? Many people do, confusing the exhilaration of speed during the journey with satisfaction upon arrival. Time management is much more about balance and satisfaction in life. Not wasting time on nonessentials so that you can do something more meaningful with your time is far more important than getting there first.

SOURCE: *Get a Life Without Sacrificing Your Career* by Dianna Booher (McGraw-Hill, 1996).

only load up the next day with unexpected and unscheduled tasks.

Keep a record on your calendar of who you called back and when. If you spend too much time playing phone tag with someone, send him an e-mail instead; calling him repeatedly might be bothersome to him and it takes up your time.

Stating your availability clearly. One way to limit interruptions from incoming calls is to state clearly that your available time is limited. When asked whether you have time to chat, say, "I have two minutes. Shoot." Don't give false excuses or lie, such as telling a caller you have to run to a meeting when you don't have to. You have important work in front of you and don't need to apologize for excusing yourself to get back to it.

> "There are a few things that you can do that will yield better results than your doing a whole lot of other things . . . and it's your duty to yourself and your team to know where your highest payoff activities are and eliminate activities that yield the fewest results."
>
> —David Cottrell,
> author of *Monday Morning Mentoring*

Don't give people on the telephone—or in person—openings for lengthy conversations. If a person refuses to specify what he wants during a phone call, ask, "What can I do for you?" If he won't get to the point, help him by saying, "I need to sign off now. Before I go, is there anything else I can help you with?" If he doesn't jump to the point right then and there, he didn't have one.

Keeping yourself focused helps you keep others focused, especially during a phone call. If what's being discussed doesn't move something forward in a palpable way, shift the focus until it does.

People who may feel like chatting in the morning or at midday are less likely to be chatty around five o'clock. If you need to cut off a lengthy description of their weekend at the lake, ask politely if you can call back to hear the end of the story, then call back about 4:45. The rest of the lake saga will probably be brief.

AGENDAS SQUEEZE OUT THE SMALL STUFF

Avoid getting bogged down in the small stuff, particularly during meetings. Well-thought-out agendas help you and the meeting attendees focus on the "vital few" ideas rather than the "trivial many." They help everyone keep their eyes on the prize. Setting the proper agenda is half the battle when it comes to running efficient meetings.

SOURCE: *Defeating Procrastination* by Marlene Caroselli (Skillpath Publications, 1997).

THE BOTTOM LINE

Red Flags ⚑◆

THE PERILS OF TAKING WORK HOME

One of the most insidious time traps you can fall into is the belief that by working a little longer, or by taking work home on the weekends, you can finally catch up. Face it: Work can, and will, consume all of your free time if you let it. You need to draw the line and maintain a healthy balance between your personal life and work. Each must have its limits.

SOURCE: *The Complete Idiot's Guide to Managing Your Time* by Jeff Davidson (Alpha, 2001).

Making efficient calls. Offer the same courtesy to people you call that you'd like them to extend to you. Begin the call by telling the person on the other line that you understand she is busy and you will only take a few minutes of her time. Even if the person you're calling is not too busy to chat, she will take your cue—you have courteously indicated that you need to get down to business. Truly busy people will appreciate your consideration. Before you make a call, think about the points you need to cover.

When leaving a message on someone else's voice mail, always note what you're calling about. A clear message will help you stick to an agenda when your call is returned.

Avoid Inefficient Meetings

Meetings—face-to-face events and teleconferences alike—can be great consumers of collective time. While it's often important to meet as a group to get work done, it's equally important to conduct meetings in a timely fashion. To run a productive meeting, preparation is key. You need to make sure there's a valid reason for the meeting and that the right people are invited.

Purpose. Determine what you want to accomplish at the meeting. Let everyone know in advance why their presence is required, what their roles are, and how their participation fits into the big picture.

Never waste time at the beginning of a meeting deciding what should be on the agenda. Prepare and distribute an agenda in advance. When participants know the overall agenda, they come better prepared, leaving more time during the meeting to move the group's thinking forward.

People. Who needs to be involved? Inviting people to a meeting who don't really need to be there wastes their time—as well as everybody else's—by bringing up unrelated issues. When you invite people to a meeting, always tell them why you have asked them. For example, tell George in Finance, "We need a financial services representative to advise us on the fiscal boundaries related to this project." If you can't tell a person precisely why he is needed at a meeting, don't extend the invitation. (If you are asked to a meeting that you have no reason to attend, politely decline.)

Let those invited know how much you expect them to contribute. You might tell Jill from human resources, "As our human resources representative, will you please report on the staffing needs of this project?" The advance notice gives Jill the chance to do some research or to hand the request off to someone else. Having the right person at the right meeting is a first step to ensuring meetings will be more productive and time efficient.

"An organization in which everybody meets all the time is an organization in which no one gets anything done."

—Peter Drucker

Time and place. What's the best venue for the meeting? Should it be on- or off-site? A teleconference or online? Although logistics often dictate the answer, your goal should always be to minimize the impact the meeting will have on your and other people's time. Be considerate of the attendees' time constraints—asking someone, for instance, to meet you off-site might

Dos & Don'ts ☑

WELL-RUN MEETINGS

If they are not run efficiently, meetings can easily consume inordinate amounts of your valuable time.

- ☐ Don't call a meeting unless you have a good idea of what you want to accomplish in it.

- ☐ Do consider carefully who should be invited to the meeting.

- ☐ Do cancel the meeting if key decision makers can't be present.

- ☐ Don't plan the agenda at the beginning of meeting; prepare and distribute it ahead of time so people arrive focused.

- ☐ Do start the meeting on time.

- ☐ Don't wait for latecomers to begin the meeting.

- ☐ Do keep track of time and ensure all items in the agenda are discussed.

- ☐ Do be considerate of attendees' time constraints when calling an off-site meeting.

- ☐ Do end the meeting on time.

• POWER POINTS •

MANAGING MEETINGS

Meetings can turn into incredible time-wasters. They can also be an effective use of time, especially when it comes to exchanging real-time information and getting real-time feedback. Make the most of your meetings by:

- Having a clear purpose to be productive

- Distributing an agenda in advance

- Planning logistics to minimize disruption

be a nice idea, but not necessary to get your task accomplished. Indeed, it may be a time sinker for both of you, and a teleconference would be more convenient and time efficient.

Meeting manners. Start on time—don't let latecomers derail the meeting agenda and schedule even before the meeting has started. Once a meeting begins, get people quickly into meeting mode. If half the room is distracted by their cell phone or handheld wireless devices, ask them to put their electronic gadgets aside for the remainder of the meeting, unless such tools will be specifically needed. Monitor the time you spend on each item on the agenda and keep moving the conversation toward a resolution. Always end the meeting on time. If the meeting is running over its allotted time, invite people to continue the conversation, but give them the chance to leave if their schedules don't allow them to stay.

When you promise to get people in and out promptly and give them ample opportunity to prepare for a meeting, you've set the best possible stage for accomplishing the purpose of the meeting in a time-efficient manner.

Stop Excessive Chatting in Its Tracks

Of all the time traps in the workplace, one of the biggest is distracting conversations. Chatting or engaging in casual conversation with coworkers is a natural part of the work day—and sometimes necessary to build strong relationships between colleagues. Still, excessive casual conversation can gobble up minutes and hours of your valuable time.

Adopt some conversational phrases to put a stop to it. When someone comes to your office door unannounced, don't be rude and wave them off. Look up, smile, and say, "Good to see you. I'm in the middle of something, but I've got about two minutes to hear what's up with you." You've now established a parameter that the other person has to respect, and you've announced exactly how much time you can give.

Don't cut people off—simply let them know up front that you're guarding your time. Your comments force a brevity that wouldn't otherwise be there. People learn quickly and will stop trying to engage you in lengthy conversations.

Dos & Don'ts ☑

DEALING WITH DISTRACTION

The best way to get over the little hurdles in your day that eat up your precious minutes is to fully acknowledge that distractions happen. The faster you admit you have been derailed, the faster you can correct the issue and get back on track. While there is no magic to eliminating distractions, they can be dealt with easily and without too much damage if handled properly.

- ☐ Do set aside a certain amount of time for responding to e-mail and returning telephone calls.

- ☐ Do keep e-mail messages succinct and to the point, but friendly none-theless.

- ☐ Don't forward jokes and junk e-mail to others, especially if you yourself find them a waste of time.

MAINTAINING A HEALTHY RHYTHM

Even if things are going smoothly and you are practicing effective time-management techniques, don't let yourself get complacent. If you are ahead of schedule on a project, don't waste

- [ ] Don't allow telephone calls to turn into lengthy conversations that drain precious time away from more important tasks.

- [ ] Don't feel bad about cutting phone calls or other coworkers short when you are working on something important.

- [ ] Do let others know that you are busy, but don't forget that others are too. Mutual understanding of time constraints will make things run more efficiently.

- [ ] Don't let office chatter become a time-consuming distraction. Let others know up front that you are busy but willing to hear what they need to say.

- [ ] Do be mindful and respectful of other people's time and schedules.

precious time by slacking off. Instead, keep going at your typical pace. In fact, the time to step on the gas is when you're ahead of schedule, not when you're behind. When your back is to the wall, you can't properly negotiate for the things

• POWER POINTS •

STAY FOCUSED AND IN RHYTHM

Allowing yourself to become too casual at work can cause you to slip into poor time-management practices. On the other hand, pressing too hard can burn you out. Develop and maintain a good tempo by:

- Avoiding casual conversations at work that will put you behind schedule
- Letting people know up front that you're consciously guarding your time
- Knowing when to step on the gas or ease off to meet deadlines for what's on your list
- Scheduling mini-breaks and vacations to establish the pace you want for your health

you need—such as more resources—because you're in a position of weakness. It's like trying to accelerate in a car that badly needs a tune-up.

However, be aware of burnout. If you are efficient and self-disciplined, you may be proud of your ability to accomplish a great deal—and you might well take on too much, determining that anything and everything requires your utmost attention. The truth is that by doing too much, you might be under-producing and wasting valuable time. That's because, by overloading your time, you can quickly wear yourself out. You may even inadvertently isolate yourself from, or alienate, people with whom you could develop the synergy to produce at an even higher level.

In fact, taking care of yourself is so important that you should not leave it to chance. Schedule mini-breaks throughout the day, and go some place where you can't be interrupted. Plan weekends so that you don't wind up on Sunday evening wondering when the recreation is going to begin. Don't overlook the restorative and regenerative effects of vacation time on your body and your spirit.

Sound time-management practices are intended to make you more—not less—in control of both your life and your work. By aggressively protecting your work time—scheduling your activities and planning ahead—you can then afford to keep your work and personal life in balance.

Some of the most productive people and best time managers are not the superhumans who can work around the clock and bounce back for more. They are the ones who establish an even pace and trot along at a moderate rate of efficiency. Like the tortoise, they get to the finish line in good shape, having done good work.

TIME MANAGEMENT IN THE WORKPLACE

"I am miserly with my time in some areas so that I can be profligate with my time in other areas."

—Stanley Marcus,
cofounder of Neiman-Marcus (1905–2002)

You're on your way to mastering the use of your own time. Now you need to consider how your time is affected by others. In an office, no worker is an island. Building a workplace in which time management is a priority not only improves everyone's productivity, but also creates an environment of respect.

Self-Assessment Quiz

**TIME MANAGEMENT:
PROBLEM OR SOLUTION?**

Read each of the following statements and indicate whether you agree or disagree. Then check your score and study the analysis at the end.

1. When I'm offered more money to work additional hours, I try to negotiate a solution based on improved time management rather than simply more hours.

   ○ Agree
   ○ Disagree

2. When I'm offered the opportunity for promotion if I work additional hours, I try to negotiate a solution based on improved time management rather than simply more hours.

   ○ Agree
   ○ Disagree

3. When I'm offered the opportunity to gain more prestige by working additional hours, I try to negotiate a solution based on improved time management rather than simply more hours.

○ Agree
○ Disagree

4. When I am not offered anything to work additional hours, I am reluctant to work beyond my designated work week.

   ○ Agree
   ○ Disagree

5. When I'm offered the opportunity to work additional hours for no particular gain, except to help out a coworker I respect, I'm willing to work beyond my designated work week.

   ○ Agree
   ○ Disagree

6. When I'm pressured to work additional hours for no particular gain, except to help out a boss I don't like, I try to negotiate a solution based on improved time management rather than simply more hours.

   ○ Agree
   ○ Disagree

Self-Assessment Quiz

7. When I'm offered the chance to work fewer hours, even if it means making less money, I strongly consider the benefits of more personal time.

   ○ Agree
   ○ Disagree

8. When I'm offered the chance to work additional hours and my family doesn't want me to, I refuse to give up any family time to work.

   ○ Agree
   ○ Disagree

9. When I'm given the opportunity to work additional hours, I feel my first obligation is to myself, my family, or my friends.

   ○ Agree
   ○ Disagree

10. If I am given the opportunity to work extra hours on a project that will benefit my personal growth or directly benefit my family, I jump at the chance to do something meaningful for people I care about.

○ Agree
○ Disagree

Scoring

Give yourself 2 points for every question you answer "Agree" and 1 point for every question you answer "Disagree."

Analysis

10–13   You might be in serious need of money and seek out every possible chance to rack up overtime, no matter what else it costs you in life. This could be a result of poor time management, money management, or both. You might also derive all or most of your sense of self-worth from the work you do. You could also be too timid to say "No" to authority figures. Whatever the reason, if you scored in this range, your actions are signaling a potentially serious problem with your time management.

Self-Assessment Quiz

14–17 You have a fairly well-balanced approach to work and life. You are susceptible, however, to manipulation by bosses who will gobble up time that would otherwise be yours. Beware of being talked into doing tasks that will eat up your valuable time. At some point, you will need to decide what you truly value and reflect that in how you choose to use your time

17–20 You understand that more can be done in less time

Indeed, respect and focus are both at the heart of managing time—both yours and that of others. Being considerate of the time of your subordinates, coworkers, and boss requires as much discipline as protecting and organizing your own time. Encouraging people to remain focused on goals and tasks that are critical to the business—and to dedicate their time to accomplishing those goals—can be a challenge.

RESPECTING OTHER PEOPLE'S TIME

Perhaps the best way to gauge how important it is to respect the time of others is to think of how you feel when a boss, coworker, or subordinate through time management. You also have a strong sense of boundaries between work time and personal time. More than that, you don't tend to derive your personal identity or sense of self-worth from the work you do. You value your personal time as well as your relationships with family and friends. You do run the risk of being too detached from work and not balancing your time adequately.

wastes your time—especially when you're at your busiest. Colleagues impose demands on your time every day: by sending confusing messages or setting unclear expectations, chatting about irrelevant topics, calling unnecessary meetings, and being late to meetings. And in turn, you need to be aware of how you may be imposing demands on other people's time.

Communicating Efficiently

To be respectful of other people's time, it is critical to become a good communicator. If you cannot clearly communicate a message, you might send a coworker on a wild goose chase that squanders

"If concentration provides the energy and attention needed for right action to take place, and discrimination (prioritizing) provides the attention and standards needed to know what action needs to be taken, then organization provides the room for right action to take place."

—Michael E. Gerber,
author of *E-Myth Mastery*

her precious time. If you don't communicate expectations clearly to your subordinates, they might misinterpret your directions and waste efforts on unnecessary tasks. If you take 20 minutes to explain a simple issue to your boss, the next time something comes up he might be reluctant to meet with you, knowing you will take up more of his time than you need to.

When composing an e-mail or leaving a message, take the time to structure your thoughts

CASE *FILE*

THE TIME LOG

When former World Bank chief economist and U.S. Secretary of the Treasury Lawrence H. Summers taught at Harvard, his students complained about not having enough time. So he taught them about time logs. He had them write down the amount of time they spent on each activity each day: sleeping, eating, writing papers, playing sports, and so on. The students were able to understand just how they spent their time, then use that information to make some changes.

Many other management gurus and successful businesspeople keep time logs. For instance, the late Peter Drucker strongly advised using them. And former Chick-fil-A president James L. S. Collins found the practice so helpful that he never gave it up.

SOURCE: *Time Tactics of Very Successful People* by B. Eugene Griessman (McGraw-Hill, 1994).

Outside the Box

PUT ON AN ACTION ATTITUDE

Time can get the best of you—or you can get the best of time. To make time work for you, action is required on your part.

If something is bothering you, speak out and do something about it—don't procrastinate. Change what you can change; let go of what you can't change—quickly. When you feel yourself tensing up, breathe deeply, take a break, and cool off. A few moments to collect yourself can save you from making wrong, time-wasting decisions. When you make a mistake, don't waste time by dwelling on it. Move on as soon as possible.

When you're criticized, take only what fits and leave the rest. When you're about to criticize someone, stop before you waste your time and theirs. When disputes arise, don't waste time trying to prove you're right; instead look for common ground—it's there.

Remember, any time you save is time for you.

first and prune out extraneous information. Don't pour your message out in a stream-of-consciousness style. Keep your communications short and to the point, while remaining friendly. Coworkers will appreciate your brevity. If you think certain e-mails are a waste of time, chances are your peers do, too. If forwarded joke e-mails seem pointless, don't forward them yourself.

When calling someone, let him know you won't take more than a few minutes of his time. He will be relieved that you are taking his time seriously and will be more likely to be responsive to your conversation.

Be aware of other people's verbal and non-verbal cues. If someone doesn't immediately engage in casual conversation when you walk into her office, realize that she might be trying to focus on an important task and doesn't want to be interrupted. When you walk into someone's office uninvited, don't immediately launch into a discussion; instead, ask if this is a good time to talk and be respectful of the person's answer. If she responds that it isn't a good time, don't insist; ask her if you can schedule some other time to talk.

When you communicate with your boss, be especially mindful of time. Some people get so little attention from their bosses that they hoard it when they finally have it. But if you suffocate your boss, she will be impatient with you for not valuing her time. Before meeting with your boss, make a list of issues you want to cover and mentally outline your conversation. Pay attention to your boss's signals to determine how much information and detail she likes. Then deliver it, stay on point, and move the conversation along briskly. You want to provide prime information in optimal time. Your boss might not consciously know that you are respecting her time, but she will be glad to keep her door open to you.

In meetings, be the one who asks the time-factor questions when dealing with projects, particularly with other departments. Saying, "I know everyone's time is valuable," or "I know that your time is valuable," sends a clear message that you respect others' time and don't intend to

• POWER POINTS •

COMMUNICATING WELL TO SAVE TIME
Nothing shows that you respect other people's time as much as the way you communicate:

- Be brief in your written communications, especially e-mail.

- Always let people you call know you won't take more than a few minutes of their time—and then keep to your promise.

- Avoid barging into someone's office; instead ask the person if this is a good time to talk—and respect their answer.

- Be especially mindful of your boss's time. Don't hoard it!

waste it. That will certainly be appreciated. More importantly, you will also be taking a leadership role in the use of time and resources—a proactive and respectful stance that people will come to identify with you.

> "I don't care how much power, brilliance or energy you have, if you don't harness it and focus it on a specific target, and hold it there you're never going to accomplish as much as your ability warrants."
>
> —Zig Ziglar

Being on Time

"Be on time from sun up to sun down," say old-school time managers. Poor time-management practices almost always affect your daily schedule. If you fail to accurately estimate how long it takes to accomplish what you have to do and to build in time to deal with unexpected interruptions, you probably won't be able to keep to your schedule. As a result, you'll get behind in your tasks and, before you know it, you will be late—for an appointment, a meeting, a conference call, or an important deadline.

Being punctual is a gesture of respect for the other person's time. But the person your lateness hurts the most—especially if you're habitually late—is you. Being known as a punctual person

The BIG Picture

FOCUSING ON THE RIGHT THINGS

Time management and organization are among the most widely taught skills in corporate training. The problem with some time-management instruction is that it typically concentrates on teaching people how to get things done more effectively. But unless you consistently focus on identifying and doing those things that have a substantial impact on your job or that are important to you, being better organized could end up filling your time with meaningless or unimportant tasks that will make you more frustrated in the long term.

SOURCE: *The 10 Natural Laws of Successful Time and Life Management* by Hyrum W. Smith (Warner Business Books, 1995).

Behind the Numbers

WHAT'S YOUR TIME WORTH?

We can all benefit from reframing our sense of time. How can you lead one successful hour after another? Put it in numbers:

- A person earning $30,000 per year is earning roughly 30 cents per minute, or about $18 per hour.

- A person earning $50,000 per year is earning roughly 50 cents per minute, or about $30 per hour.

- A person earning $75,000 per year is earning roughly 75 cents per minute, or about $45 per hour.

- A person earning $100,000 per year is earning roughly $1 per minute or about $60 per hour.

If you wrote yourself a mental check at the end of every day for the minutes and hours you used effectively, what would it total? If you billed yourself for the minutes and hours wasted, what would the amount be? Would you wind up with a net profit or loss for the day?

SOURCE: *Leadership When the Heat's On* by Danny Cox with John Hoover (McGraw-Hill, 2002).

is a plus if you want to position yourself as a superior time manager.

To be punctual, you need to make a habit of planning ahead. When you are planning to catch an airline flight, you don't just check your departure time the morning you are supposed to leave; you check a day or so before to decide when you should leave for the airport and how you will get there. Why should planning to arrive on time at meetings be any different? Plan for meetings ahead of schedule by setting time reminders in your calendar and allowing plenty of time to get to the meeting place.

Also, you can't keep your day on schedule— and help others keep their schedules as well—if you come out of a meeting late. If a meeting

Dos & Don'ts ☑

PUNCTUALITY RULES

Being punctual to meetings and appointments not only reduces time wasting but is also a powerful way to demonstrate your respect for other people's time.

☐ Do plan ahead by setting reminders in your calendar.

☐ Do arrive a few minutes early to meetings and appointments.

☐ Don't start meetings late for late arrivals.

runs long, excuse yourself once the main business is completed, explaining that you have another commitment. Ask someone to take notes on the balance of the meeting for you. You can also end an appointment by tactfully, but firmly, excusing yourself. You're a manager with a mission now, and that doesn't include running late.

Be particularly vigilant about respecting your boss's time, even if he is constantly wasting yours. When your boss is expecting you at two o'clock, be a few minutes early—even if that means you have to wait. It's not up to you to decide that what you're doing is more important than meeting with your boss. If your boss is chronically late, make sure you come

- [ ] Don't derail your schedule by coming out late from meetings. If the meeting is running long, excuse yourself.

- [ ] Do be vigilant about being on time to appointments with your superiors.

- [ ] Don't assume your team members know the importance of punctuality. Remind them frequently that punctuality increases productivity and reduces stress in the department.

prepared—and that he comes prepared—by letting him know ahead of time the agenda for the meeting, so he can consolidate his thinking before you meet. You can gently remind him about the meeting by asking, "Is there anything else I can prepare to make the two o'clock meeting run more smoothly?" If your boss is still late to your meeting, at least being prepared might speed up your discussion and ensure that the meeting is productive and ends on time.

When you are on time, you are also setting an example for your staff. Don't assume your people know how to be punctual. Remind them that starting and ending meetings promptly is important and that restarting meetings for late arrivals wastes everybody's time. It's also disrespectful of those who showed up on time. Ensuring that your subordinates are routinely punctual reduces time-wasting throughout your department.

Setting an example of good time management and respect for other people's time is critical. Start by explaining why and how you value your time. Remember that the way you protect and make the most effective possible use of your time—and theirs—sets a standard for those under you. If you consistently demonstrate the behavior you want your employees to adopt, your example will be effective.

The same thing is true with your peers. Although you lack the institutional power to effect changes in how your coworkers manage their time, you can encourage them to be on time to meetings and appointments, especially meetings you are attending together, by sending them short and friendly reminders. There are always circumstances beyond your control. But to the degree that you can plan and execute your schedule, being punctual (overcoming bad habits if necessary) will benefit both you and others.

Staying Focused

Staying focused means learning to shelve tasks that don't require your immediate attention, to

• POWER POINTS •

FOCUSED ON TIME

Even the best time-management skills won't help you much if you focus on the wrong tasks. A superior time-management plan helps you decide what is the best investment of your energy. Remember:

- Good time management helps you to focus on the task at hand.

- Sharing your agenda is a good way to let folks know when to leave you alone.

- Learning to say "No" to time wasters is like buying extra time.

- Focusing on time management means you're focusing on your work.

manage other people's demands by sharing how you are using your time, and to say no when appropriate.

This doesn't mean ignoring everything that pulls you from your task—you don't want to

STAYING FOCUSED ON TIME MANAGEMENT

Fostering respect for other people's time is the first step to nurturing an organization committed to making the most of the time available. Still, saving time is not of much use if people focus whatever time they've saved on the wrong tasks. The key to effective time management is focus.

When you are focused on a goal or task, your mental and physical energies are all applied to achieving it. Concentrating and keeping a clear focus on your goals, tasks, and priorities helps you fend off the interruptions and demands from others that threaten to derail you from succeeding. When you are focused, you are in control of your time: You know what's important, you know what your priorities are, and you know how to put those priorities first.

THE BOTTOM LINE

become isolated and lose sight of what's going on in the workplace around you. The point of being focused is not to completely tune out distractions, but to manage them.

If poor time-management habits have allowed distractions to derail your goals, then focusing can put you back on track. When you are asked to take on extra work, for example, make it clear that your availability depends on the priorities you are currently focused on. "I'll certainly try to help," you say, turning to your schedule. "Let me see where that fits into my agenda."

KEEPING YOUR TEAM FOCUSED

When your team members are tearing their hair out, you can be reasonably assured that their time-management skills are lacking and they are not focusing appropriately. Their failure to accomplish goals and tasks becomes your failure. You need to step in and help them learn to focus on the right things and to manage distractions.

As the boss, you are the one who ultimately has the responsibility to be a good steward of all resources—especially time—available to you and your department. That means doing whatever you can to improve the efficiency and the time-management skills of the members of your group. One way to approach that goal is to remember the saying that the best way to learn something is to teach it. The smartest thing you can do to help everyone improve their time-management techniques is to teach each other. You can take both a macro and micro approach

• POWER POINTS •

TIME MANAGEMENT IN ACTION FOR TEAMS

If the members of your team are not in control of their time, their productivity and efficiency will suffer. Here are a few ways to improve your team's time-management skills:

- **Lead by example** – Be the first to enroll in time-management training. Put the techniques you learn into practice.

- **Keep everyone aware that time is important** – Respect other people's time and urge them to respect yours.

- **Create a time-management plan for your team** – Discuss ways in which the whole group can eliminate time-wasting efforts.

- **Match the right person to the right job** – When an employee's natural abilities are not aligned with his job, boredom and restlessness set in, leading to wasted effort.

- **Organize your work area** – How you allocate your space—assign work areas and place filing cabinets and storage space—can significantly affect your group's productivity and efficiency.

to encouraging your team to adopt positive time-management skills.

Macro Approach

Create a time-management plan. When you focus on time management in your department, you and your staff begin supporting each other in a joint effort. Discuss ways to prevent time wasting in areas of your department that

> "There's never time to do it right, but there's always time to do it over again."
>
> —Meskimen's Law

seem especially inefficient. Set up an informal forum, in which your staff can share their time-saving tricks. Some people have a natural sense of how to use time effectively, and everyone can benefit from their wisdom. Don't forget to offer your own suggestions. Then draft a time-management plan that allows everyone to focus on tasks and objectives that support the company's goals.

Assign time-management responsibility to everyone on your team, but don't forget that as the person in charge, you must lead by example. You don't need to become a time monster and ride everybody relentlessly. People are human

Plan

SLOW DOWN TO SAVE TIME

Good time management doesn't necessarily mean leaping into action. Playing fast and loose with decisions might work in the short run, but too many poor decisions, made in haste, can turn out to be penny-wise and pound-foolish. Patching that hole in the loading dock door with duct tape might be a quick fix, but taking the time to repair it correctly—perhaps even installing a new door—will save much more time later. When confronted with a problem, take the time to write down all your available solutions and alternatives. Before making a decision, consider the value of the time that will be saved in the long run by adopting a solution that may be slower but will be permanent.

SOURCE: *The 25 Best Time Management Tools and Techniques* by Pamela Dodd and Doug Sundheim (Peak Performance Press, 2005).

Behind the Numbers

TIME, MOTION, AND OUTPUT
Time and motion studies are used to help some businesses maximize efficiency. Time studies record the time it takes to perform each task in order to establish time standards for every job. Motion studies analyze each movement made in accomplishing each task. Although it might seem tedious to study time and motion so closely, it is the only way to determine the most efficient sequence of actions and establish standards upon which to predict business performance and growth potential.

SOURCE: *The Small Business Handbook* by Irving Burstiner (Fireside, 1997).

and they may wiggle a little on their time-management plans. If you're too tough on them, your people will resent you and begin to abdicate responsibility. Define benchmarks to monitor your group's collective progress toward the completion of tasks, objectives, and goals. Continuously review how time could be better used. Make updates on your time-management plan a priority.

Sharpen your organizational skills. Once you've begun to set priorities and organized your

Behind the Numbers

YOU ARE LESS PRODUCTIVE THAN YOU THINK

How many of your workday hours are genuinely productive in terms of producing revenue? How many are spent commuting, filling out paperwork, attending meetings, dealing with vendors, and in other such activities? One study of Fortune 500 CEOs revealed that CEOs spend an average of 28 truly productive minutes per day.

SOURCE: *No B.S. Time Management for Entrepreneurs* by Dan Kennedy (Entrepreneur Press, 2004).

people to function in the most time-efficient manner possible, step up your organizational-design skills. Making sure that all employees in your department are placed in the right position for their skills can save precious time in the long term. When a person's natural talents and abilities are not aligned with his job, boredom, restlessness, and resentment can set in. As a result, his time is squandered. The more people are misaligned, the more complex your time-management challenge. Putting your people to work at tasks that are aligned with their own abilities and that complement their colleagues ensures that you're achieving maximum efficiency from the time you have.

Learn from other departments. If you work closely with another department that is operating on a different calendar or schedule from yours, talk to your counterparts in other areas and find out how you can compare schedules and coordinate plans to maximize efficiency

CASE *FILE*

ORGANIZERS BUILD ORGANIZATIONS

Evidence suggests that the key people at formative stages of visionary companies exhibited a stronger organizational orientation than those at comparable, but less-than-visionary, companies, regardless of their personal leadership styles. For instance, Jack Welch played a huge role in revitalizing GE, making reorganization a high priority.

Among other things, Welch's leadership saved the company's ailing locomotive division, and it rocketed to the top of the industry. In GE shops, locomotives were repaired and put back in service faster and less expensively than ever before. The locomotive team's results were truly astonishing. Superior organization saved time and turned a greater profit.

SOURCE: *Built to Last* by Jim Collins and Jerry Porras (HarperBusiness, 2004).

Dos & Don'ts ☑

TIME MANAGEMENT AND THE ORGANIZATION

Good time management seldom just occurs on the spur of the moment. What you want to accomplish must be thought out in advance and planned carefully.

☐ Do consider the time efficiency of your whole group.

☐ Do create a time-management plan for yourself and your department.

☐ Don't forget your use of time is setting an example.

☐ Do be punctual and respect other people's time.

☐ Don't ignore the time-planning tricks you can learn from your employees or other departments.

☐ Do organize your work area to maximize efficiency.

between departments. You can also learn from their best practices and find out about how they focus their energies and efforts and manage their time to achieve greatest efficiency. How do they value time relative to their organization's financial performance? Their protocols might

- [ ] Don't work so fast and furiously that the quality of your work suffers.

- [ ] Do plan and strategize how you can help your boss be more time efficient.

- [ ] Don't allow your boss's poor time-management habits to derail your schedule.

- [ ] Do assign time-management responsibility to members of your team.

- [ ] Don't waste other people's time with meaningless assignments.

- [ ] Don't allow intrusions and distractions to rob your time-management focus.

shed light on ways that you waste time, effort, or resources. The more information you share among work groups, departments, areas, or organizations, the stronger the foundation you are laying for an integrated time-management effort across the company.

Micro Approach

Organize your work area. How you organize your team's space can also help them save time and stay focused on their goals as well as those of your company. Psychologists have recently found

• POWER POINTS •

ORGANIZE AND RECOGNIZE

It's easy to believe that if you're running at full throttle you must be getting a lot done. You might be wasting time looking for things that better organizing skills would have made more accessible. When people demonstrate good organization and time-management skills, don't let it go unnoticed.

- Keep your work space well-organized to help people move quickly and efficiently.

- Rid your physical space of clutter to make information easy to access.

- Coach your people into good organizing habits and watch for progress.

- Be sure to recognize people who show good time-management and organizing skills.

Outside the Box

THE SPACE ATTACK

Organizing expert and author Julie Morgenstern developed the SPACE plan for attacking clutter and organizing your physical environment:

Sort – Sort things into groups of similar items.

Purge – Toss it, give it away, sell it, put it in long-term storage—but get it out of your working space.

Assign a Home – Things you've decided to keep need a place. Be efficient with your storage: Consider size, accessibility, safety, and sequence of use.

Containerize – Containers keep categories of items separated and make retrieval, cleanup, and maintenance easy.

Equalize – Monitor your bins, shelves, wall units, and drawers. When something doesn't work, make a change. If you begin accumulating again, "attack" your SPACE.

SOURCE: *Organizing from the Inside Out* by Julie Morgenstern (Owl Books, 2004).

that cubicles with higher partition walls tend
to give workers a "rat in a maze" complex, while
lower walls encourage a freer exchange of ideas.
When organizing your project teams, bear in
mind that their geographical space will affect the
time it takes to get them to work together.

> "The job of negotiating a mutually satisfactory agreement about time is part of the manager's job."
>
> —John Kao,
> author of *Jamming*

In order for your organization to move quickly
and efficiently, you need to make sure that data
and information are disseminated among team
members and other critical players at an optimal
level. Physically configuring your team's work
space will affect their agility. Filing systems,
both physical and digital, should suit the needs
of your team and be flexible and adaptable.
De-cluttering is often cited as a surefire way to

become more time efficient. The critical issue is not aesthetics, but the accessibility of data: Someone who can quickly find what she needs in a mountain of clutter is better off than someone whose work space is neat as a pin but must search for hours to find anything.

To heighten awareness of time management among your team, it's also vital to instill a time-management awareness and a sense of focus in each individual. Remember, the chain is only as strong as its weakest link. Monitor every individual's progress toward adopting the time-management plan. In one-on-one meetings or coaching sessions, review your team members' to-do lists and ask questions about how their plans fit into the department's plans.

Finally, make special recognition possible for people who demonstrate the best time-management techniques. Then spread the word. Offer incentives to workers who suggest better time-management approaches to assignments, tasks, projects, and initiatives. Anticipate that people might actually have extra time, and be prepared to help them find ways to use it wisely.

KEEPING YOUR BOSS FOCUSED

Most workers are occasionally exasperated by their boss's lack of concentration. The higher someone moves up the corporate ladder, the more distractions he has to deal with. But as the single most important player in your working life, your boss exerts the most control and demands over your time. You are in a bind if he is terrible at focusing and managing time.

Your ability to influence your boss's ability to focus time-management skills or at least keep his weakness from diminishing your own effectiveness takes finesse and diplomacy. You can't force him to change. But there are things you can do to improve the situation.

First, ask yourself where your boss goes wrong: What does he do that wastes time? Does he cause delays and disruptions by losing information? Does he assign tasks to the wrong people?

Behind the Numbers

RATIO ANALYSIS

To determine how efficient you are, check the relationship between your time and income. If you earn $400 for a 40-hour week (about $10 per hour), the ratio of your income to an hour of your time is 10 to 1. If you get a 25 percent raise, the ratio might seem to increase to 12.50 to 1. But the promotion may mean spending more time at work. If you spend 80 hours a week at work but are compensated for 40, the ratio becomes 12.50 to 2. Promotions can be expensive, unless you learn how to manage your workload and time better. As you climb the corporate ladder, it is important to become more time efficient.

• POWER POINTS •

PERSONAL CHANGE

Time-management skills can be learned. They can even be practiced with self-discipline. But true time management must become a way of life, if you expect to derive all of the benefits it has to offer you personally and professionally. Don't forget that:

- Serving customers faster, more cheaply, and better occurs with good time management.

- Saving money and resources by doing things right the first time is a result of good time management.

- Working on time-management skills with subordinates and peers will build stronger relationships.

- Using better time-management techniques can begin right now.

Does he ignore incremental deadlines? Does he wait for a task to become a crisis before it snags his attention? If any of this affected him alone, it wouldn't be your problem. If you can anticipate your boss's distractions and time-management weaknesses, you will be better prepared to deal with them.

Outside the Box

LEARNING ABOUT YOURSELF FROM OTHERS

Why is your boss's negligent behavior so irritating? Do you have the same habits? It's often hard to endure faults in others that you see in yourself. At the same time you're studying your boss, also consider how you manage your time at work. For instance, do you, too, wait to take action until things have reached crisis proportions? By noting your own time-management flaws in someone else, it's easier to see how to improve them.

If it's hard to get your boss's attention in the office, try to meet off-site, perhaps over a meal. If you get him away from his desk and work distractions, you'll have a greater chance to get him to focus on you and your needs and accomplish more in a shorter period of time. If you know he often takes long to give authorization or sign off on projects, build extra time in your schedule to account for your boss's lack of speed. If he doesn't articulate his thoughts clearly in impromptu meetings, provide him with a well-thought-out agenda in advance of your conversation so he has a chance to collect his thoughts.

Even if you can't influence what your boss focuses on, you might be able to engage his help in removing obstacles or roadblocks that are affecting your team's ability to focus on the right goals and tasks. If anybody will understand the profit and performance payoffs that flow from the ability to focus, it will be your boss.

By diplomatically working around your boss's flaws and practicing good time-management skills, you can lighten the load for you and your boss—and enhance your market value. Plus, learning to cope with an inefficient boss can make your workplace far more tolerable. It's no lie that workers "don't leave bad jobs, but flee from bad bosses."

COMMITTING TO PERSONAL CHANGE

Getting a handle on time management can be an overwhelming proposition. Yet imagine having control over your time and workload. Imagine saying "no" to your inner workaholic. Imagine saying "no" to your subordinates, peers, and superiors who make inappropriate demands on your time. Imagine saying "no" to the minutiae that threaten to overwhelm you.

Now that you've learned to prioritize your tasks, stay focused, avoid distractions, teach your subordinates to manage their time, and work around your boss's time-management deficiencies, you are in the best position to finally gain control of your time. Focus on eliminating wasted time or effort, refusing work that doesn't move your agenda or your company's forward, keeping track of your projects, and staying on top of your to-do lists. In so doing, you will positively affect not just your time-management habits, but those of other people in the organization.

The Case for Time Management

Time is one of your most valuable assets and needs to be managed well if you are to make the most of it. The difference between successful managers with bright futures and unsuccessful managers who stay stuck in one spot usually has less to do with their intelligence or skill level and more to do with how effectively they manage their time. If you want to begin moving up faster in your career, start by improving the way you manage your time.

You can become the poster child for productivity, the champion of time efficiency—not by nagging but by being alert to opportunities to serve internal and external customers faster, cheaper, and better. You can use every opportunity your peers offer to organize your mutual space and working relationships. With your boss, you can become the go-to person who relieves departmental pressures by getting it done right the first time and on time.

Setting and enforcing time-management habits isn't easy and can't be done in an instant. Chances are that what is really standing in your way is a lack of self-discipline. Changing behavior is difficult—but incredibly rewarding. And it is most successfully achieved by small, incremental, manageable steps. You've heard the mantras: "A journey of 1,000 miles begins with a single step," and "You climb a mountain one rock at a time." If you really want to manage your time better, recognize that, yes, it will take a major effort to overcome the inefficient habits that have become ingrained. But it is also true that the first step to change may be as easy as getting out a piece of paper and starting your to-do list right now.

Off and Running >>>

You are now ready to put what you have learned from this book into practice. Use this section as a review guide.

CHAPTER 1.
PRIORITIZE YOUR TIME

- Everybody gets the same hours in a day: It's really a matter of how you use them.

- Good time management brings benefits: Increased daily output, meeting career and financial goals, and better opportunities for success are all possible.

- Be more efficient with your time: Efficiency in the present will help you achieve what you want in the future.

- Prioritize according to your body clock: See when you are most efficient at making decisions or focusing on work and devote that time exclusively to those tasks.

- Don't overwhelm yourself: Take big tasks and subdivide them into smaller tasks. Remember, a journey of a thousand miles begins with a single step.

- Understand the big picture: This will help you stay focused and prioritize better.

- Always keep priorities in mind: Unimportant things usually become urgent because of bad planning.

- Write things down: Even those with steel-trap minds sometimes forget important details or items that need attention.

- Don't get bogged down: Prioritize your list and focus on the most important items.

- Make a list on a computer or digital planner: You'll always be able to find it and can update it more quickly. If you must cross-out items on your to-do list, print out a copy and mark it up.

- Remember the real object of time management: Use the time you have efficiently rather than cutting corners to save time at any cost.

- Time management helps creativity: Rather than wasting time maneuvering through chaos and disorder, good time management opens up

Off and Running >>>

space in your life, allowing more time for the creative process.

- Know where your list is and keep it there: Jotting things down on backs of envelopes and loose pieces of paper won't help you progress; you'll just waste time looking for that scrap with that great idea.

CHAPTER 2.
ORGANIZE YOUR TIME

- Don't reinvent the wheel: Use templates and already created forms or e-mail signatures so you do not have to write the same thing over and over again.

- A good schedule is flexible: That way, unforeseen developments and complications can be accommodated.

- Have a Plan B: This will ensure that you don't spin your wheels when things go awry.

- Do it now: Use those pauses throughout the day to get the little things that need doing done.

- Give yourself enough time: Remember incidentals in your day such as e-mails and taking and returning phone calls. Activities you forget to include in your schedule can wipe out the extra time in the margins of your day.

- Don't be afraid to complete tasks "out of order": The important thing is to maximize resources and key players.

- In a pinch, hire a temp: Sometimes with deadlines looming, there's too much to do, and it's time to call in some reinforcements.

- Oil the squeaky wheel: Figure out what is slowing you down to get things moving again.

CHAPTER 3.
USING YOUR TIME EFFICIENTLY

- Avoid e-mail distractions: Don't read every e-mail right away; designate a specific time of day for handling them. Delete or file them away after you've replied or otherwise dealt with the content.

Off and Running >>>

- Manage the phone trap: Screen your calls when you are focusing on an important project; then return them in their order of importance.

- Set agendas for meeting: Everybody has things to do; stay on course and finish the meeting sooner rather than later.

- Start meetings on time: This will avoid wasting valuable time waiting for late comers and signals that timeliness is a priority.

- Maintain a healthy rhythm: Don't be complacent, don't slack off—keep it going.

- Don't burn yourself out: Know when to step on the gas or ease off to meet deadlines.

CHAPTER 4.
TIME MANAGEMENT IN THE WORKPLACE

- Build a workplace where time management matters: This improves everybody's productivity and creates an environment of respect.

- Communicate effectively: relating information clearly will save everybody involved time and effort.

- Don't dwell on mistakes: Everybody makes them; change what you can change and proceed.

- Respect other peoples' time: Don't ramble, interrupt somebody on deadline, or take more of your boss's time than she wants to give.

- Be punctual: The person your lateness hurts most—especially if you're habitually late—is you. Remember, a punctual person is a walking advertisement for superior time management.

- Stay focused: Learn to shelve things that don't require your immediate attention.

- Keep your team focused: Help them learn to focus on the right things and manage distractions.

- Create a time-management plan: Draft a plan that allows everybody to focus on tasks and objectives that support the company's goals.

Off and Running >>>

- Sharpen organizational skills: Aligning a person's natural talents and abilities with his job ensures his and your department's success.

- Learn from other departments: Compare schedules and coordinate plans to maximize efficiency.

- Organize your work area: Decluttering and organizing can help your team stay focused on goals.

- Give recognition to those who demonstrate the best time-management techniques: Public praise is a good impetus for reinforcing positive behaviors.

- Learn about yourself from others: Seeing your own time-management flaws in somebody else makes it easier to see how to correct them.

- Be committed to making change permanent: Prioritize tasks, stay focused, avoid distractions, teach your subordinates to better manage their time, and work around your boss's time-management deficiencies. Staying the course will improve your life.

Recommended Reading

The One Minute Manager Meets the Monkey
Ken Blanchard
This step-by-step guide by best-selling author
Blanchard shows managers how to free themselves from doing everyone else's jobs and
ensure that every problem is handled by the
proper staff person.

*Putting the One Minute Manager to Work: How
to Turn the 3 Secrets into Skills*
Ken Blanchard
The second book in this phenomenally
successful series shows how to apply the tenets
of the *One Minute Manager* to one's day-to-day
existence to bring out optimum efficiency.

*The On-Time, On-Target Manager: How a "Last-
Minute Manager" Conquered Procrastination*
Ken Blanchard and Steve Gottry
In this engaging parable, Blanchard and Gottry
offer practical strategies any professional can
put into practice to improve his performance

and transform himself from a crisis-prone Last-Minute manager into a productive On-Time, On-Target manager.

Get a Life Without Sacrificing Your Career
Dianna Booher
Booher offers time-saving tips and argues that setting realistic expectations and the right goals are key to establishing priorities that align with one's personal values.

The Small Business Handbook
Irving Burstiner
This is a comprehensive nuts and bolts guide to starting and running a small business that covers topics from making the decision to start a business to managing employees.

Defeating Procrastination
Marlene Caroselli, Ed.D.
This book presents 52 tips (one a week for a year) to help readers choose progress over procrastination and includes exercises to help improve productivity and efficiency.

Good to Great: Why Some Companies Make the Leap . . . and Others Don't
Jim Collins
The findings from *Good to Great* will surprise many readers and shed light on virtually every area of management strategy and practice.

Leadership When the Heat's On: 24 Lessons in High Performance Management
Danny Cox with John Hoover
In *Leadership When the Heat's On,* former test pilot Danny Cox discusses how to adapt the results-driven characteristics of fighter pilots

to any organization and presents strategies for optimum efficiency in today's fast-changing workplace.

How to Get Organized When You Don't Have the Time
Stephanie Culp
Culp offers an easy-to-follow five-step program to get organized for busy people.

The 25 Best Time Management Tools and Techniques
Pamela Dodd and Doug Sundheim
This short but comprehensive book presents the best of what time-management experts have to offer.

The Daily Drucker: 366 Days of Insight and Motivation for Getting the Right Things Done
Peter F. Drucker with Joseph A. Maciariello
Widely regarded as the greatest management thinker of modern times, Drucker here offers his penetrating and practical wisdom with his trademark clarity, vision, and humanity. *The Daily Drucker* provides the inspiration and advice to meet life's many challenges.

The Effective Executive
Peter F. Drucker
Drucker shows how to "get the right things done," demonstrating the distinctive skill of the executive and offering fresh insights into old and seemingly obvious business situations.

The Practice of Management
Peter F. Drucker
The first book to depict management as a distinct function and to recognize managing as a separate responsibility, this classic Drucker work

is the fundamental and basic book for understanding these ideas.

The E-Myth Revisited
Michael E. Gerber
The original best seller is revised, with more
information on why so many small businesses
fail and what you need to know to run a successful business.

The Power Point
Michael E. Gerber
The author of the best-selling E-Myth series
examines the biggest companies in their fields
and shows how they stay on top.

Time Tactics of Very Successful People
B. Eugene Griessman
Griessman offers a collection of time tactics
used by a variety of highly successful people
such as Malcolm Forbes, Jr., and Ted Turner.

*It's Not the Big that Eat the Small . . . It's the
Fast that Eat the Slow: How to Use Speed as a
Competitive Tool in Business*
Jason Jennings and Laurence Haughton
This instructive text tells how to create strategic
planning and creativity to speed your business
efficiently past the competition.

"Yes" or "No": The Guide to Better Decisions
Spencer Johnson, M.D.
Best-selling author Spencer Johnson presents a
practical system anyone can use to make better
decisions in both one's professional and personal
life.

*What Really Works: The 4+2 Formula for
Sustained Business Success*
William Joyce, Nitin Nohria, and Bruce Roberson
Based on a groundbreaking 5-year study, analyzing data on 200 management practices, *What
Really Works* reveals the effectiveness of practices that really matter.

Time for Me: A Burst of Energy for Busy Women!
Helene Lerner
This parable illustrates how working women need
to take time out from taking care of everyone
and everything else in order to make time for
themselves to become more efficient in the long
run.

Organize Your Work Day in No Time
K. J. McCorry
This book shows how simple time-management
techniques can help managers and employees
do their work in less time.

*Managing Crises Before They Happen: What
Every Executive and Manager Needs to Know
about Crisis Management*
Ian I. Mitroff and Gus Anagnos
The heads of the consulting firm Comprehensive
Crisis Management give tips and advice on heeding the warning signs, thinking outside the box
to devise coping strategies, and learning from
previous debacles to plan for the future.

*Organizing from the Inside Out: The Foolproof
System for Organizing Your Home, Your Office,
and Your Life, 2nd edition*
Julie Morgenstern
Organizational expert Julie Morgenstern teaches
readers how to organize their work space

and offers solutions that are tailored to the individual's habits and personality.

In Search of Excellence: Lessons from America's Best-Run Companies
Thomas J. Peters and Robert H. Waterman, Jr.
Based on a study of 43 of America's best-run companies, *In Search of Excellence* describes eight basic principles of management that made these organizations successful, along with providing helpful advice on getting things done.

Quiet Leadership: Six Steps to Transforming Performance at Work
David Rock
Rock demonstrates how to be a quiet leader, master at bringing out the best performance in others, by improving the way people process information.

The 10 Natural Laws of Time and Life Management
Hyrum W. Smith
Smith, vice chairman of the board of FranklinCovey, explains the natural laws that govern time management and explores how by organizing your time, you'll organize your life and derive a sense of satisfaction and well-being from doing so.

Leave the Office Earlier: The Productivity Pro Shows You How to Do More in Less Time . . . and Feel Great About It
Laura Stack
Stack introduces readers to ten productivity factors and presents an individualized and effective approach to getting organized.

*The Cycle of Leadership: How Great Leaders
Teach Their Companies to Win*
Noel M. Tichy
Using examples from real companies, Tichy
shows how owners and managers can begin to
transform their own businesses into teaching
organizations and, consequently, better-perform-
ing companies.

*The Leadership Engine: How Winning Companies
Build Leaders at Every Level*
Noel M. Tichy
A framework for developing leaders at all levels
of an organization helps to create the next gen-
eration of leaders so that a company can grow
from within, which is the key to excellence,
stability, efficiency, and the building of team
loyalty.

Winning
Jack Welch with Suzy Welch
The core of *Winning* is devoted to the real
"stuff" of work. Packed with personal anecdotes,
this book offers deep insights, original thinking,
and solutions to nuts-and-bolts problems.

Getting Organized
Stephanie Winston
Considered one of the classics in the field of
organization and time management, this best
seller offers tips on how to organize time, paperwork, financial records, and meals, along with
setting priorities, getting rid of clutter, and
teaching organizational skills to children.

The Organized Executive: A Program for Productivity—New Ways to Manage Time, Paper, People, and the Electronic Office, Revised Edition
Stephanie Winston
Winston reveals how to analyze organization needs, optimize performance, end paper build-up, increase productivity, and combat procrastination.

Index

Make sure you have all the Best Practices!

Best Practices: Achieving Goals
ISBN: 978-0-06-114574-2

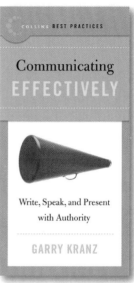

Best Practices: Communicating Effectively
ISBN: 978-0-06-114568-1

Best Practices: Difficult People
ISBN: 978-0-06-114559-9

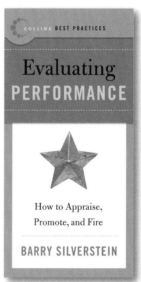

Best Practices: Evaluating Performance
ISBN: 978-0-06-114560-5

Make sure you have all
the Best Practices!